Anonymous

Knitting and Crochet

An Illustrated Manual of Home Industry

Anonymous

Knitting and Crochet
An Illustrated Manual of Home Industry

ISBN/EAN: 9783743423510

Manufactured in Europe, USA, Canada, Australia, Japa

Cover: Foto ©Lupo / pixelio.de

Manufactured and distributed by brebook publishing software
(www.brebook.com)

Anonymous

Knitting and Crochet

New-York Tribune.

EXTRA, NO. 62.   **20 CENTS.**

KNITTING AND CROCHET,

AN ILLUSTRATED MANUAL

OF

HOME INDUSTRY,

CONTAINING

PLAIN, PRACTICAL DIRECTIONS FOR MAKING A

LARGE VARIETY OF

USEFUL AND ORNAMENTAL ARTICLES,

FANCY STITCHES, ETC.

CONTENTS.

INTRODUCTION.

The hearty enthusiasm with which the first number of the Knitting Extra was received, the large number sold, and the anxious inquiries as to its successor, have determined THE TRIBUNE to publish the second number as soon as possible. The shape has been altered to one which it is known will be more convenient and acceptable to its fair readers, and more easily preserved. As a handy pamphlet giving a carefully-selected variety of patterns, in clear type and good paper, with appropriate illustrations, this publication is absolutely unique. Its price will be 20 cents. For 25 cents both this and the first Knitting Extra, No. 59 (the regular price of which is 10 cents), will be forwarded to any address.

ERRATA.

CORAL AND LEAF EDGING.—Page 37, 5th row: Insert "2 plain, over," at beginning, before "3 plain." For "1 plain," the first time it occurs, read "3 plain," and insert "over" after the next "1 plain."

WHEAT-EAR EDGE.—Page 27, 8th row: For "purl 2 together" read "purl 5 together."

PRACTICAL DIRECTIONS IN KNITTING AND CROCHET WORK.

TERMS IN CROCHET.

After careful comparison of the most competent foreign authorities and of the patterns sent to this department from domestic sources, it has been determined to change the code of terms in crochet hitherto used, and make it conform to that most in use among our subscribers. Accordingly, the stitches in all crochet patterns which are hereafter to appear will be the various stitches which are explained below. It will be seen that they are very simple and easily understood.

SINGLE STITCH OR SC.—Put the needle in a stitch of the work, bring the cotton through in a loop, and also through the loop on the needle.

DOUBLE CROCHET OR DC.—Put the needle in a stitch of the work, bring the cotton through; take up the cotton again and bring it through the two loops.

TREBLE STITCH or TC.—Turn the cotton round the needle, put it in a stitch, bring the cotton through; then take it up and bring it through two loops twice.

LONG STITCH OR LONG TREBLE.—Turn the cotton twice round the needle, work as the treble stitch, bringing the cotton through two loops three times.

EXTRA LONG STITCH.—Turn the cotton three times round the needle, work as the treble stitch, bringing the cotton through two loops four times.

It is probably not necessary to explain "chain" to anybody, as it is the foundation of all crochet and is simply a straight series of loops, each drawn with the hook through the preceding one.

KNITTED EDGINGS.

"Housekeeper" contributes the following charming patterns. She says: "I enclose directions for knitting two edgings; these narrow edges for ruffling, etc., are of more practical use than the wider patterns, though very little variety can be afforded within the limits of four, five or six stitches."

No. 1.—SINGLE EYELET SCALLOP.—Cast on 6 stitches.

1st row—1 plain, thread over twice and purl 2 together, knit 1, thread over three times and knit 2.

2d row—Knit 3, purl 1, knit 2, thread over twice and purl 2 together, knit last 1 twist stitch.

3d row—Knit 1, thread over twice and purl 2 together, knit 6.

4th row—Cast off 3, knit 2, thread over twice and purl 2 together, knit 1 twist stitch.

No. 2.—BIAS EYELET POINT.—Cast on 4 stitches.

1st row—Knit 2, thread over and knit 2 together, thread over and knit 1.

2d row—Knit 5 plain.

3d row—Knit 2, thread over and knit 2 together, thread over and knit 1.

4th row—Knit 6 plain.

5th row—Knit 3, thread over and knit 2 together, thread over and knit 1.

6th row—Cast off 3 and knit 3 plain.

DEEP LACE.

(Mrs. A. S. Stephens.)

Materials—Cotton No. 40, crochet hook No. 22. Make the chain the required length.

First row: * 7 chain, miss 5, 1 double on the 6th, repeat from *.

Second row: * A double on centre of the 7 ch., then 7 ch. and repeat.

Third to seventh rows: Like the second. (These rows may be all worked backward and forward.)

Eighth row: * 1 double in centre of the 7 ch., five chain, and repeat from *.

Ninth row: 1 double on centre of 5 ch., *3 ch., miss 2, 1 DC (double crochet) on 3d ch., miss 1, 1 DC on second; repeat from *.

Tenth row: 1 SC on the beginning of the chain (a), * 3 chain, miss 2, 1 DC on 3d; repeat from * twice; 6 chain, slip stitch on same stitch, 6 chain, slip stitch on same stitch, and repeat from (a). (Slip stitch is made by putting the hook through the stitch and drawing the cotton at once through it and the loop on the hook.)

Eleventh row: 1 DC on centre of 6 ch., 6 ch., 1 DC in centre of next 6 ch., 5ch., 1 DC on centre of 3 ch., 5 ch., 1 DC on centre of next 3 ch. Repeat.

Twelfth row: * 3 longs under 6 ch, 3 longs under next 6 ch, then 12 ch, and repeat from *.

Thirteenth row: 6 TC on 6 longs * 3 ch., 1 DC in 3rd ch, repeat from * four times; then repeat from beginning.

Fourteenth row: 6 TC in 6 of last row, * 5 ch,

1 DC under 3 ch., repeat from * five times; then repeat from the beginning.

Fifteenth row: 6 TC into the last 6, * 6 ch., 1 DC under 5 ch. of last row, repeat from * four times; then repeat from the beginning to the end, and fasten off.

GENTLEMAN'S VEST.

This may be knitted in black, single Berlin wool with two needles, No. 12, with a knitted border of violet wool. The fronts are done in the pattern to be described; the back in brioche stitch. For carrying out the work the best plan is to cut a paper pattern as a guide for the size and shape of the knitted pieces, and work strictly to pattern. In

At the end of the row knit 1 twist, 1 purl, 1 twist. Sixth row: 1 purl, 1 plain, 1 purl, * 1 plain, 2 purl, 1 plain, 1 purl, 1 plain, 1 purl, repeat from *. These six rows repeated compose the pattern. Its peculiarity is that it knits two totally different patterns on the two sides of the work, and the knitter can choose which she prefers. To make openings for the pockets as many stitches as are necessary must be cast off and replaced in the next row by casting on an equal number. If the pattern on the wrong side is used these stitches must all be cast off plain, not purl, in the second and fourth rows. When you have reached the armholes, cast off on that side in different rows as may be required by your pattern the necessary number of stitches to shape it, and then continue the front

measuring the depth and width of the fronts, allowance must be made for the border, to be knitted afterward, of 15 rows of ribbed knitting.

The piece for each front is begun at the lowest edge by casting on 73 stitches (each repetition of the pattern takes 7, and 3 are added at the end to make both edges uniform). First row: * 1 twist stitch, 1 purl, 1 twist, 1 purl, 2 plain, 1 purl, repeat from * ; at the end of the row add 1 twist, 1 purl, 1 twist (the twist stitch is a plain stitch knit from the back part of the loop). Second row: 1 purl, 1 plain, 1 purl, * 1 plain, 2 purl, 1 plain, 1 purl, 1 plain, 1 purl, repeat from *. Third row: like the first. Fourth row: like the second. Fifth row: 1 twist, 1 purl, 1 twist; of the next 4 stitches knit the fourth first plain and pass it over the three others (to facilitate this pass the point of the right hand needle into the stitch as if about to purl it, and loosen it by drawing it forward before knitting it); then do the same to the second of the four stitches, knitting it plain and passing it also over the first, then knit the third in like manner, and finally knit the last stitch also plain. Repeat from *

till you slope it for the shoulder and neck of the pattern.

For the back cast on 110 stitches and knit in brioche stitch as follows, after one purl row : First row : Take off one stitch *, thread forward, slip 1, as if about to purl, knit the next stitch plain, and repeat from *. Second row : * thread forward, slip, as if about to purl, knit the next stitch and the 'thread forward' of the last row together, and repeat from *. If there is a stitch left at the end knit it plain, and slip in the next row as in the first row. The second row is repeated till the back is high enough to slope for the shoulder. In taking in stitches at the beginning of the rows on each side for this purpose, knit the stitch and thread forward always as one stitch. The fronts and back must now be sewn together at the shoulders and sides.

For the border, 4 or 5 needles, No. 12, will be required. Pick up the stitches all along the lower edge of the vest, knitting them one by one as you take them up (like the heel of a stocking), and place as many on a needle as it will conveniently hold. With these rib 15 rows, 1 plain, 1 purl, increasing 1 at the beginning of every row for the mitering at the corners, and cast off. Now take up the stitches down both fronts and around the neck in the same manner, and rib the same number of rows, increasing one at the beginning of each for the corners. In the border of the left front 7 buttonholes must be made at regular intervals by casting off 3 or 4 stitches, replacing them in the next row by casting on an equal number. When the 15 rows of ribbing are done, cast off, and without breaking the wool, pick up the edge stitches of the sloped corners of one front and the waist each on a needle, and knit them off together, taking a stitch from each needle at a time, and then cast them off. This will form the miter neatly. Every corner must be finished in the same manner. Then pick up the stitches around the armhole on three needles, knitting them as you take them up, and ribbing them to correspond with the rows of the border. The pockets of twill gray lining are then to be put in, the outer edge of the vest bound with black braid, and buttons sewn on the border of the right front,

This completes the vest.

BED SPREAD (*KNITTING*).

Mrs. J. C. W., of Flushing, sends the following simple but very pretty pattern for a knitted bed-spread:

Use No. 8 Dexter cotton 3 thread, and medium sized knitting needles—steel.

Cast on 3 needles 8 stitches; 3 on 2 needles, and 2 on a third; with a fourth needle join in a circle and knit once around plain; every alternate row is to be knit plain:

2d row: Make 1, knit 1, and repeat round the entire row.

4th row: Make 1, knit 2, and repeat all round.

6th row: Make 1, knit 3, and repeat all round.

8th row: Make 1, knit 4, and repeat all round.

10th row: Make 1, knit 5, and repeat all round.

12th row: Make 1, knit 6, and repeat all round.

14th row: Make 1, knit 7 and repeat all round.

16th row: Make 1, knit 8, repeat all round.

18th row: Make 1, knit 1, make 1, knit 2 together, knit 6, repeat all round.

20th row: Make 1, knit 1, *make 1, knit 2 together, repeat from * once, knit 5, repeat all round.

22d row: Make 1, knit 1, *make 1, knit 2 together, repeat from * twice, knit 4, repeat all round.

24th row: Make 1, knit 1, *make 1, knit 2 together, repeat from * 3 times, knit 3, repeat all round.

26th row: Make 1, knit 1, *make 1, knit 2 together, repeat from * 4 times, knit 2, repeat all round.

28th row: Make 1, knit 1, *make 1, knit 2 together, repeat from * 5 times, knit 1, repeat all round.

30th row: Make 1, knit 1, *make 1, knit 2 together, repeat from * 6 times, repeat all round.

32d row: Cast off until only 17 stitches remain.

The remainder is knit with 2 needles. (In knitting across the first row, take up a loop and knit it, so that there will be 18 stitches instead of 17.)

1st row: *Knit 3, purl 3, repeat from * to the end of the needle.

2d and 3d rows: Like the 1st row.

4th row: *Purl 3, knit 3, repeat from * to the end of the needle.

5th and 6th rows: Like the 4th row.

7th, 8th and 9th rows: Like the 1st.

10th, 11th and 12th rows: Like the 4th row.

13th, 14th and 15th rows: Like the 1st row.

15th, 17th and 18th rows: Like the 4th row. Cast off the last row. This completes one piece. It takes about 250 pieces for a quilt.

KNITTED LACE.

Mrs. L. M. T. is good enough to send the following directions for a pretty lace: Cast on 19 stitches,

1st row: Slip 1, knit 1, over, narrow (knit 2 together), knit 1, over twice, narrow, knit 5, over, narrow, over, narrow, over, narrow, knit 1 (twist).

2d row: Slip 1, 13 plain, 1 purl, 2 plain, over, narrow, 1 plain (twist).

3d row: Slip 1, 1 plain, over, narrow, 9 plain, over, narrow, over, narrow, over, narrow, 1 plain (twist).

4th row: Slip 1, 16 plain, over, narrow, 1 plain, (twist stitch).

5th row: Slip 1, 1 plain, over, narrow, 1 plain, over twice, narrow, over twice, narrow, 4 plain, over, narrow, over, narrow, over, narrow, 1 plain (twist stitch).

6th row: Slip 1, 12 plain, 1 purl, 2 plain, 1 purl, 2 plain, over, narrow, 1 plain (twist).

7th row: Slip 1, 1 plain, over, narrow, 11 plain, over, narrow, over, narrow, over, narrow, 1 plain (twist).

8th row: Slip 1, 18 plain, over, narrow, 1 plain (twist stitch).

9th row: Slip 1, 1 plain, over, narrow, 1 plain, over twice, narrow, over twice, narrow, over twice, narrow, 4 plain, over, narrow, over, narrow, over, narrow, 1 plain (twist).

10th row: Slip 1, 12 plain, 1 purl, 2 plain, 1 purl, 2 plain, 1 purl, 2 plain, over, narrow, 1 plain (twist).

11th row: Slip 1, 1 plain, over, narrow, 14 plain, over, narrow, over, narrow, over, narrow, 1 plain (twist).

12th row: Cast off 6 loosely, leaving 18 stitches on left hand needle, 15 plain, over, narrow, 1 plain (twist stitch).

This completes the pattern. Begin again at 1st row.

KNEE CAP.—Miss Jane Rowley sends directions for knitting a knee-cap on two needles. It can be made larger or smaller by widening or not. Cast on 23 stitches, knit garter stitch until you have about half a finger-length. Then knit as follows: 1st row: Knit 9 stitches, then make 2 stitches out of the 10th titch by knitting the stitch, but not taking it off the left needle. Then put your needle in the back part of loop and make a stitch. Knit the rest plain. 2d row: Knit 9 stitches, then widen by making 2 stitches ont of one as in first row, then knit plain to end. Repeat this till you have fifty stitches inside of the 9 edge stitches, and knit about 20 rows without widening for the top of the knee cap. Then begin and narrow by knitting 2 together on each alternate side the same way you widened. When you have it narrowed to 23 stitches, knit half a finger-length like the beginning and sew together.

KNITTED SOCK.

Mrs. A. D. H. writes:

I have enjoyed and profited so much from the patterns of the knitting column, that I wish to add something that may help others. I inclose a little sock pattern, given me some time since by a friend, which I have found both useful and pretty:

Materials—One ounce each of blue zephyr (single) and Saxony yarn, four common coarse knitting-needles.

Cast on with zephyr 46 stitches. First row plain, 2nd row purl, 3d row plain; then join yarn; 4th row plain; 5th row purl.

6th row: Knit 1, narrow twice,* over, knit 1, over, knit 1, over, knit 1, over, narrow four times *, repeat till but five stitches remain, narrow twice, knit 1.

7th row purl; 8th row plain; 9th row purl; 10th row the same as 6th row. Repeat 7th-10th inclusive till you have six rows of holes, from top of sock, making 26 rows in all.

27th row purl; 28th purl; then join zephyr, 30th plain; 31st plain; then join yarn; 32d row plain; 33d row purl.

34th row: knit 1 * over, narrow, * repeat to the end of the row. 35th row, purl. 36th plain, 37th purl, join zephyr. 38th plain, 39th plain, join yarn. 40th row, plain; 41st purl. 42d row, knit 15 stitches, then with a third needle knit 1, narrow, over, knit 1, over, knit 2, narrow twice, knit 1, over, knit 1, narrow, knit 1, leaving fifteen stitches on the needle from which you have been knitting. The third needle contains 16 stitches, which are the foundation for the top of the foot, and on these knit with the fourth needle. 43d row, purl. 44th row, plain. 45th, purl.

46th same as 42d. Repeat 42d–45th inclusive till you have five rows of holes, making 58 rows. 59th row, purl. 60th row, plain, 61st row, purl, join zephyr and knit 20 rows plain, then narrow at beginning and end of each alternate row till but ten stitches remain. Now with the needles containing each 15 stitches, pick up stitches on sides of the foot, and you now have on 1st and 2d needle each about 48 stitches and 3d needle 10 stitches. On these 3 needles knit all around six rows plain. Now narrow at end of 1st needle, middle of 2nd (or centre needle) and beginning of 3d needle,

every alternate row till but 3 stitches remain on centre needle, divide these, putting one on 1st needle, two on 3d needle, make the number of stitches equal by narrowing, narrow at beginning and end of each needle each alternate row till you have knit six more rows. Lay the two needles together and cast off. Join the back in a seam. Press, and running a colored ribbon or cord and balls in the row of holes made by 34th row, the sock is completed.

NARROW EDGING (CROCHET).

The first Vandyke of this pretty edging is made thus: Make a chain of 15 stitches. First or centre row: Turn, miss the last 2 chain, and work 2 DC.; 2 treble ; 2 long ; turn on the wrong side leaving 7 chain.

2d row: Make 6 chain; miss 3; 1 DC. on the centre row; 4 chain ; miss 2; 1 DC. in the point of the centre row; 5 chain, 1 DC. in the same stitch

of the point as before; 4 chain, miss 2, 1 DC. on the other side of the centre row ; 4 chain, turn on the right side, join to the 5th stitch of the 7 chain that were left.

3d row: Miss 1 and in the last 4 chain work 1 DC., 1 chain, 2 treble, 4 chain, 2 treble, 1 chain and 1 DC.

These DC and treble stitches are all to be worked in the same loop of chain. Repeat 4 times more in each loop of chain.

For the second Vandyke work as the 1st to the end of the 2d row ; then

3d Row—Miss 1, and in the last 4 chain, work 1 DC., 1 chain, 2 treble, 2 chain; join to the last 4 chain of the 1st Vandyke; 2 chain and in the 4 chain as before, work 2 treble, 1 chain, 1 DC. Then * miss 1, and in the next 4 chain, work 1 DC., 1 chain, 2 treble, 4 chain, 2 treble, 1 chain, 1 DC. Repeat from * 3 times more. Work on as the 2d Vandyke, until your edging is of sufficient length.

SHELL STITCH FOR CHILD'S STOCKING.

P. A. S. very kindly sends directions for a shell stitch pattern for a stocking, as follows:

Cast on each needle any number of stitches that is a multiple of 14, as 28, 42, 56.

It may perhaps simplify the directions if I say now that the following order of knitting produces rows of shells bounded on each side by a row of seamed stitches. These shells in their widest part, the middle, include 9 stitches, and at either end one stitch.

1st round : Knit 9 stitches plain. This is the foundation for the first shell which can only be a half one, because of the necessity of commencing in the middle of it. Every alternate shell at the beginning of the stocking will be similarly incomplete. Seam 2, knit 1. This last is the foundation stitch for the second shell, and it must be remembered this is to be the centre stitch of the shell and that the increasing shall each time take place on either side of this stitch. Indeed, if properly knitted, this stitch can be traced continuously through the row of shells from top to heel. Seam 2, knit 9, and proceed as before.

2d round : The 1st shell and every alternate one now must begin to decrease. Therefore, slip 1st stitch, knit 2d, and slip 1st over it, leaving only 8 stitches before the two seamed ones. Knit these 8, seam 2, and as the second shell and every alternate one must now begin to increase, leave the thread in front of the needle and knit the next stitch. Throw the thread twice about the needle from front to back, and seam the next two stitches. This shell has now increased from one to three stitches, because a loop has been formed either side the foundation stitch.

Now slip one again, knit one, and slip the first over the second, as already stated for the first shell.

3d round same as 1st, only the second shell on each needle and every alternate one will have 9 stitches to knit instead of 1. The first shell and every alternate one will decrease one as usual.

4th round same as 2d, only that in the second shell and every alternate one, after the centre stitch is knitted the thread needs to be brought only in front of the needle, and not twice about it as when this centre stitch lies next the seaming stitches.

Thus the first shell, and every alternate one around, decreases one stitch every round. The second shell, and every alternate one, increases two every alternate round. When each respective shell has reached its maximum of nine stitches or minimum of one stitch, it must decrease or increase, according to the process given." The writer adds: "I hope I have made this intelligible to those desirous of patterns for fancy stockings. If not, I shall be glad to try to make myself better understood. The pattern is lovely enough to warrant quite an amount of trouble."

CLOVER-LEAF EDGING.

This is a charming little crocheted edging, and the hearty thanks of THE TRIBUNE are herewith offered to Mrs. F. M. Gideon, who presents it as follows:

With thread and an appropriately fine crochet hook make a chain the required length of the edging. Turn, miss 1, 3 treble in three successive stitches of the foundation: 7 chain, turn, 1 treble in the third chain; this forms a loop. Turn this over and work 4 chain, 1 treble in the loop, 3 chain, 1 treble in the same loop, 4 chain, 1 DC. in the same loop in the last chain stitch next the base or where it was joined to make the loop. This makes 4 loops.

Turn work over, begin in the last loop and make 1 DC. 1 half treble, 3 treble, join this (SC.) to the first long treble of foundation. Then 3 long treble, 1 treble, 1 DC. in the same loop. This completes the first leaf or lobe.

In the next make 1 DC., 1 half treble, 6 treble, 1 treble, 1 DC. Make in the third same as second.

In the fourth 5 DC. on the next 3 chain, 6 DC. This completes the leaf and stem.

Then work 6 trebles on the foundation chain. Begin with 7 chain, etc., etc., as before.

The second leaf is made same as first and is joined as follows : The middle of first leaf or lobe (SC.) to third treble last made on foundation chain, as given in the preceding. The centre of second lobe is joined between the third and fourth of the preceding leaf.

The "half" treble is made by putting thread around hook, drawing it through the stitch, catching it again and pulling it through all the three loops on the needle at once, instead of at twice as in a full treble. The sample of the edging she sends is so exquisitely pretty that subscribers are advised to spend some pains over the pattern; they cannot help but be pleased with it.

BABY'S KNITTED HOOD.

Mrs. C. Petersen, with many kind words which THE TRIBUNE appreciates, sends her contribution in the shape of the following directions for a baby's knitted hood. "The materials are 1 skein blue or pink Berlin wool and 11 knots white fleecy; wooden needles. With the white wool cast on 69 stitches and knit back plain.

First row : Knit one, make one, knit 3 plain, repeat to end of row.

Second row : Knit plain to loop or made stitch, knit that plain also and make another, knit 3 plain, knit loop, knit 3 plain to end of row.

Third row : Knit back same as 2d row, lifting or making a stitch after every loop is knit to end of row. The "loop" is the made stitch of the previous row.

Fourth row : Plain.

Fifth row : Knit one plain, * narrow or knit 2 together, knit 2 together and pull first narrowed stitches over the last narrowed stitches; repeat from * to end of row.

Commence again at 1st row ; this is for the head-piece of hood. Knit long enough to go round the head and bind off after knitting 5th row, to finish the row of shells of which the pattern consists.

For the crown cast on 40 stitches and follow the same pattern till the piece is half the length of the head-piece.

Now cast on 50 stitches with the blue wool, and knit garter-stitch or plain across both ways until you have a piece the length of the head-piece; cast off loosely, and cover this blue foundation with the white knitted piece; tack on loosely. For the crown foundation cast on 36 stitches, and knit same as blue for the head-piece. Knit to same length as white crown-piece, cast off loosely and cover with white crown-piece. Place the end of the crown-piece in the centre of the doubled head-piece, and sew up on the right side with an over-and-over stitch.

For the border cast on 10 stitches of the blue wool, and knit garter-stitch until a piece is knitted long enough to go round the hood, and also round the seam when the crown is sewn to the head-piece. A crocheted cord of blue, with little blue balls at the end for strings to tie in front, and also to gather the crown a little at the back of the neck, completes this simple and pretty knitted hood.

I improved mine a little, I think, by putting a row of scallops all round the edge of the blue border with an ivory crochet hook, and working into every row of the garter stitch first 1 SC, 1ch, 2 DC 1ch; fasten down tight between the scallops by putting the hook through a stitch on the edge of the border. Put the wool over once, and draw it

3rd Row—Make 1 chain; miss 2; 1 DC. in the last 3 chain; 3 chain, miss 3 and 1 DC. in the 3 chain of the last row 8 times; turn back.

Repeat the last row for 7 rows more, working the "3 chain, miss 3, and 1 DC.," once less each row; then work 18 single down the side of the Vandyke to the first row even with the foundation chain; then make 25 chain and repeat from the first Vandyke until sufficient is made.

Last Row—Commence in the 1 chain worked at the beginning of the 2d row of the 1st Vandyke, and up the side work 3 chain, miss 1 and 1 DC. 8 times, 3 chain miss 1, 1 DC. in the 3 chain of the last row of the Vandyke; and in the same 3 chain 5 chain, 1 DC., 7 chain, 1 DC. 9 chain, 1 DC., 7 chain, 1 DC., 5 chain, 1 DC., in all 6 DC. in the 3 chain. Then work down other side of the Vandyke 3 chain, miss 1, and DC. 9 times; 1 chain miss 5 between the Vandyke, 1 DC. on the 1 chain at the beginning of the 2d row of the next Vandyke. Repeat along the Vandykes.

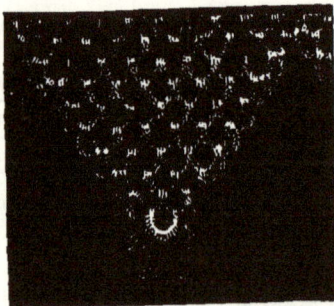

through the loop on the hook. A pleating of soft white lace round the face has a pretty, delicate effect."

VANDYKE BORDER (CROCHET).

This handsome lace is crocheted the short-way—that is, a scallop or Vandyke at a time, instead of on a chain made the required length. Short-way edgings are more interesting to most workers than long-way ones, as the pattern grows more quickly under the fingers. For heavy furniture lace in this pattern use 12-thread crochet cotton and needle No. 1. For fine lace use Boar's-head cotton No. 24 and needle No. 4.

Begin with a chain of 25 stitches.

1st Row—Turn; miss the last 5 chain and work 1 D.C.; then work 3 chain, miss 1, and 1 D.C. 9 times; turn back on the other side, leaving 1 chain.

2nd Row—Make 1 chain; miss 2; 1 D. C. in the last 3 chain of the first row; then 3 chain, miss 3, and 1 D. C. in the 3 chain of the first row 9 times; turn back.

SHELL LACE (KNITTING).

Mrs. T. R. Corbett sends the following pretty shell lace pattern, which differs sufficiently from that published in The Weekly of November 12, to make a useful variety.

Cast on 9 stitches.

1st row: Slip 1, knit 1; thread over twice and knit 2 together three times; 1 plain.

2d row: Slip 1, 2 plain, purl 1, 2 plain, purl 1, 2 plain, purl 1, 2 plain. (The purl stitch is always the second of the two made stitches.)

3d row: Knit plain.

4th row: Knit plain.

5th row: Slip 1, knit 1, thread over twice knit 2 together, 8 plain.

6th row: Slip 1, 9 plain, purl 1, 2 plain.

7th row: Knit plain.

8th row: Knit plain.

9th row: Slip 1, knit 1; thread over twice and knit 2 together twice; 7 plain.

10th row: Slip 1, 8 plain, purl 1, 2 plain, purl 1, 2 plain.

11th row: Knit plain.

12th row: Slip 1, 6 plain, slip 6 of the 7 stitches over the last knitted stitch, leaving 1 stitch upon the right hand needle; then knit 8 plain.

Repeat from 1st row.

MOSAIC PATTERN.

The remarkable skill which the osteologist and paleontologist attain is strikingly shown in the certainty with which the forms of primeval monsters have been built up from a single bone. A broken fossil in their hands becomes an extinct bird or reptile, whose form, size and mode of life are as vivid to the scientific eye as if the Neolithic age were but a thing of yesterday. A letter from a Brooklyn correspondent asks the Crochet Department to rival these experts in another field. Mrs. E. L. E. incloses the fragment of a pattern and says: "I have been trying to copy from memory a stitch with which I saw an Afghan made. I send the sample that you may know what stitch I refer to. Will you please give the directions for correctly making it, not omitting to say how to keep the work from narrowing; also how to prevent the next row of wheels from having a wrong side appearance."

The "sample" consisted of a few rows of "wheels," very nicely worked, on each side of the foundation chain, with a intervening zigzag line of what knitters would call "chain edge." This chain edge was apparently part of a series of four-sided figures, and the problem which evidently perplexed E. L. E. was how to turn her wheels into squares, or, in other words, the old problem of "squaring the circle"—a problem, by the way, which the cleverest geometers have declared impossible. True, these ancient and modern mathematicians were men. But what woman would ever confess that her copious vocabulary included such a word as "impossible"? Let Mrs. E. L. E., therefore, proceed as follows, and success, it is hoped, will crown her efforts:

For experimental purposes, make a chain of 25 stitches.

First row: Miss 3 chain, put wool around hook, and work 1 treble into the fourth chain stitch. Work 6 more trebles into the same stitch, miss 2 ch., and finish the first "wheel" with a DC on the next ch. * Miss 2 ch., work 8 trebles into the next, miss 2 ch., and finish the second wheel with a DC on the following chain. Repeat from * to end, and fasten off. The result of the first row is a series of four wheels, each composed of eight treble stitches. The wool is broken off at the end of each row.

Second row: Join the wool at the top of the first treble of the first wheel with a DC. (This treble, remember, consists of the last 3 ch. of the foundation row.) Then put wool around hook, and insert it at the back of the second treble, just below what may be called the rim of the wheel, passing under two threads, and draw the wool through. There are now 3 loops on the hook. Draw the wool through two. This leaves two loops on the hook. Put wool around again, and insert hook in the same way through the back of the third treble. Draw the wool through, catch it again and pull through two loops. There are now 3 loops on the hook. Raise another loop in the same way on the fourth treble. These are called tricotée trebles, and there are now four of them on the hook. Catch the wool and draw it through all four, and make 1 chain. This finishes the first half-square. Make 3 chain and then 1 DC between the fourth and fifth trebles of the wheel. *Now raise four tricotée trebles on the last four of the wheel, miss the DC between the wheels, and raise four more tricotée trebles on the first four of the second wheel. There are now nine loops on the hook. Draw the wool through the whole and finish the square with 1 chain. Make 3 ch. and then 1 DC between the 4th and fifth trebles of the second wheel. Repeat from * till only 4 trebles of the last wheel are left. Raise these and make a half square as at the beginning of the row, and fasten off.

Third row: Join the wool with a DC in the same stitch as in the second row, and work 12 ordinary trebles in the little hole formed at the middle of the half square by the 1 ch. Finish with a DC worked completely over the first DC of the second row. * Next work 8 treble into the centre of the first complete square and finish with a DC worked over the second DC of the previous row. Repeat from * twice, or till the half square is reached. In the centre of this half square work 12 trebles (as in the half square at the beginning of the row), and make a DC over the last DC of second row and fasten off. As the result of the third row there are now 3 wheels of 8 trebles each in the middle, and a large wheel of 12 trebles on each side.

Fourth row: Join the wool with a DC on the top of the 8th treble of the first wheel. * Raise 4 tricotée treble, miss the DC, raise 4 more on the first 4 of the second wheel, draw the wool through the whole, and make 1 ch., then make 3 ch. and finish with a DC between the 4th and 5th trebles of the second wheel. Repeat from * three times, ending with a DC between the 4th and 5th trebles of the last wheel of 12.

Fifth row: Join with a DC exactly where the 4th row was begun, and work 8 treble into the centre of the first square, and finish this wheel with a DC worked completely over the DC of the previous row. Repeat from * three times, and fasten off. There are now 4 wheels as at the end of the first row.

Repeat the 2d, 3d, 4th and 5th rows as often as may be desired. The pattern when properly worked forms a series of squares of which the sides consist of the chain edge already spoken of, with a hole in the centre from which all the stitches seem to radiate, and a row of wheels or scallops down each side of the work. Done in double zephyr wool, as all fancy patterns ought to be, the effect is handsome.

LACE FOR SACQUES.

Mrs. M. E. T. kindly sends the following pattern for knitted lace, saying: "It is very pretty knit in colored Saxony wool to trim breakfast sacques; or in white Angola or Saxony for flannel skirts." The pattern is as follows:

Cast on 15 stitches.

1st row: Slip 1, knit 1, put thread over, knit 2 together, knit 1, thread over twice, purl 2 together, thread over twice, purl 2 together, knit 1, thread over once, knit 2 together, thread over 3 times, and knit 2 together, knit 1.

2d row: Knit 2 plain, knit 1 loop, drop 1, purl 1, knit the remaining stitches plain.

3d row: Slip 1, knit 1, thread over. knit 2 together, 6 plain, thread over, knit 2 together, knit the remainder plain.

4th row: Knit across the needle plain.

5th row: Slip 1, knit 1, thread over, knit 2 together, knit 1, thread over twice, purl 2 together, thread over twice, purl 2 together, knit 1, thread over, knit 2 together. thread over 3 times, knit 2 together, thread over 3 times, knit 2 together.

6th row: Knit 1st stitch, knit 1 loop, drop 1, purl 1, knit 1 loop, drop 1, purl 1, knit remainder plain.

7th row: Slip 1, knit 1, thread over. knit 2 together, 6 plain, thread over, knit 2 together, knit the remainder plain.

8th row: Knit across the needle plain.

9th row: Slip 1, knit 1, thread over, knit 2 together, knit 1, thread over twice, purl 2 together, thread over twice, purl 2 together, knit 1, over, knit 2 together, thread over 3 times, knit 2 together, thread over 3 times, knit 2 together, thread over 3 times, knit 2 together.

10th row: Knit 1, knit 1 loop, drop 1, purl 1, knit 1, knit 1 loop, drop 1, purl 1, knit 1, knit 1 loop, drop 1, purl 1, knit remainder stitches plain

11th row: Slip 1, knit 1, thread over, knit 2 together, 6 plain, thread over, knit 2 together, knit remainder stitches plain.

12th row: Slip 1, knit 1, pass the 1st over the 2d, and repeat until 6 stitches are narrowed, knit remainder stitches plain. We have now 15 stitches and one pattern complete. Now commence again at 1st row.

In this pattern thread "over twice" before a purl stitch means, bring the thread forward and turn once around the needle.

A CROCHETED SLEEVE.

C. C. asks for directions for crocheting the sleeves of a jacket in Afghan stitch, with the quantity of Germantown wool necessary for the pair. As she fails to state either the size of the jacket or the age of the wearer, the reply must necessarily be somewhat vague. Perhaps the following may relieve her perplexities.

First ascertain from the jacket itself (which it is presumed is already made) the number of stitches around the armhole, and make a chain of the required length. Raise four of these chain stitches in the usual Afghan stitch, and work back again. Now raise these and the next four stitches of the foundation row, and work back. On next row raise these eight stitches, with four more from the foundation chain, and continue in this way to raise four stitches from the foundation chain every succeeding row till 16 stitches are on the needle; then work back. On the following row go right across and raise all the remaining chain-stitches. Next work off four. Raise these again, and work back 8 stitches. Raise these and work back 12 stitches. Raise these and work back 16 stitches. Raise these and now work back across the whole line.

The result thus far is a little gusset on each side, intended to give the sleeve the necessary slope on the top of the shoulder. From this point work on regularly till the elbow is reached. Then narrow at each side by raising the first and second stitches as one, and also the two stitches which come before the last. Narrow in this way every second row three or four times, and then every row till within an inch of the end of the sleeve. Then raise two stitches: work back. Raise four and work back On the next row raise the stitches right across. Work off two. Raise these again, and work back four. Raise again and work back right across the piece. Finish with a row of DC. Sew the edges of the piece together and the plain sleeve is complete. In raising the stitches the perpendicular veins are, of course, picked up, and in working back the wool is first drawn through one stitch and afterward through two.

The amount of wool necessary will depend on the size of the sleeve and the looseness of the work. For a little girl two ounces will be ample, while three ounces ought to make a sleeve large enough for a young lady.

NORMANDY LACE AGAIN.

"Miss M., Portland, Me.," writes: "The fair knitter whose experience with 'Normandy Lace' was recently given is deserving of much credit for her ingenuity in getting so nicely over her difficulty with it (I have tried her method and it is good). I can't agree with her, however, that the original directions were 'a' a muddle,' as there were but two errors in the whole 12 rows, viz, in the 4th and 8th rows. I was so charmed with the illustration given that I went to work at once. All went well until I was ready to work my 5th row; then on counting my stitches I found I had 20, while only 19 were called for; so I took back the 4th row and did away with one of the 'made' stitches, and went on again until I reached the 8th row. I saw at once what the trouble was there as there was no sense in 'cast off 1 plain,' so I cast off 1, and knit one plain, and got a lace that evening which pleased everyone who saw it. But the pattern was not quite perfect and I was not satisfied, but I had not ingenuity enough to dispose rightly of that superfluous stitch in the 4th row until the Knitting Department told me how. Now the pattern is perfect. It is so very handsome that I think it would be well to print the directions again, corrected. I will inclose mine, they may be of service. Will you say to the knitters that they will save their eyes very much if they will write off their directions instead of working from the closely printed columns; not all the explanations, of course, but simply directions, condensing as much as possible. I invariably do it, unless in simple patterns which are very easily mastered." The directions for the Normandy lace which Miss M. has so kindly written out are as follows:

Cast on 15 stitches.

1st row: 8 plain, knit 2 together, over, 3 plain, over, 2 plain. (This row ends with 16 stitches on needle.)

2d row: 2 plain, over, 5 plain, over, knit 2 together, 7 plain. (17 stitches on needle.)

3d row: 6 plain, knit 2 together, over, 1 plain, knit 2 together, over, 1 plain, over, knit 2 together, 1 plain, over, 2 plain. (18 stitches on needle.)

4th row: 2 plain, over, 1 plain, knit 2 together, over, 3 plain, over, knit 2 together, 1 plain, over, knit 2 together, 5 plain. (19 stitches on needle.)

5th row: 4 plain, knit 2 together, over, 1 plain, knit 2 together, over, 3 plain, over, knit 2 together, 1 plain, over, 2 plain. (20 stitches on needle.)

6th row: 2 plain, over, 1 plain, knit 2 together, over, 3 plain, over, knit 2 together, 2 plain, over, knit 2 together, 1 plain, over, knit 2 together, 3 plain. (21 stitches on needle.)

7th row: 5 plain, over, knit 2 together, 1 plain, over, knit 2 together, 3 plain, knit 2 together, over, 1 plain, knit 2 together, over, 1 plain, knit 2 together. (20 stitches.)

8th row: Cast off 1, knit 1 plain, over, knit 2 together, 1 plain, over, knit 2 together, 1 plain, knit 2 together, over, 1 plain, knit 2 together, over, 6 plain. (19 stitches.)

9th row: 7 plain, over, knit 2 together, 1 plain, over, slip 1, narrow, pass slipped stitch over, over, 1 plain, knit 2 together, 1 plain, knit 2 together. (17 stitches.)

10th row: 2 plain, over, knit 2 together, 3 plain, knit 2 together, over, 8 plain. (17 stitches.)

11th row: 9 plain, over, knit 2 together, 1 plain, knit 2 together, over, 3 plain. (17 stitches.)

12th row: Cast off 2, 1 plain, over, knit 3 together, over, 10 plain. Commence again at first row. (15 stitches.)

STRIPE FOR "AUNT MAMIE'S SOCK."

Mrs. R. A. B. writes: "I have used 'Aunt Mamie's' directions for baby socks with success and ease, and am tempted to send another stripe for the same. Though similar, it has the advantage of shorter threads on the back. Will 'Aunt Mamie' try it and pardon me for saying it is just a little prettier? I would like our invalid friend, Miss N. A.P., to try it also on her promised 'four or five pairs more,' only I fear it will increase the labor of her willing hands, by making demands for more. I have used it on the top of the little half hose worn with the first shoes, knitted of Saxony, a red vine on white ground, with the rest of the stocking red. I also reversed the colors, but the effect was not so pretty. I have used it as a stripe above top of shoe for larger children.

I would like to tell the ladies who have not tried it of the good results of shrinking yarns—Saxony, splitzephyr, etc.—before using. If they will measure the skein before and after the process they will be surprised at the result. It is easily done in a steamer or over the teakettle, and the work retains much more softness and elasticity if frequently washed. I have just lost an Aunt Mamie and a dear invalid friend, so have especially taken an interest in the two ladies above mentioned." The pattern is as follows:

The pattern requires some number of times seven stitches—in the baby socks there are 56 stitches.

1st row: * 5 white 2 red * all around.

2d row: Begin with 4 white, then * 4 red and 3 white, * the two middle red stitches over the two red of the preceding row.

3d row: Same as 2d, only begin 1 red, then * 3 white and 4 red *.

4th row: 1 red, 4 white, then * 2 red and 5 white, * exactly alike and over 1st row.

5th row: 3 white then * 2 red and 5 white *, then 2 red stitches, being over the last 2 of 5 white in preceding row.

6th row: 1 white, then like 5th row, 2 red and 5 white, the red ones being two to the right again.

7th row: All red. This is the middle row, and after trying once the pattern can be reversed without further directions.

8th row: Like 6th.

9th row: Like 5th.

10th row: 5 red and 2 white all around.

11th row: 4 white, then * 4 red and 3 white *.

12th row: 1 red, then * 3 white and 4 red * like 11th.

13th row: 1 red, 4 white, then * 2 red and 5 white,* exactly the same as 4th row.

HONEYCOMB STITCH.

M. E. C. asks for honey-comb stitch in knitting. There are several knitting patterns known by this name. Here is one:

Cast on 8 stitches for each pattern, with 4 extra (two on each side) for edge stitches.

First row: 2 plain,* slip 2 stitches off without working from the left needle to the right, 6 plain; repeat from *. Last two stitches plain.

Second row: 2 plain, * purl 6, slip the same 2 stitches as before; repeat from *. Last two stitches plain.

Third to seventh rows: Knit these alternately as first and second rows.

Eighth row: All plain, including the slipped stitches.

Ninth row: 2 plain, purl all the rest except the last two stitches, which should be knit plain.

Tenth row: All plain.

Eleventh row: 6 plain, slip 2 (as in first row), ' 6 plain, slip 2; repeat from *. Last 4 stitches plain.

Twelfth row: Same as second.

Thirteenth to seventeenth rows: alternately as eleventh and twelfth.

Eighteenth row : Like the eighth.

Nineteenth row: Like the ninth.

Begin again from the first row.

KNITTED FRINGES.

Two subscribers send specimens of knitted fringes which will be found useful for a wide range of purposes, according to the material with which they are worked.

FIRST PATTERN.

The first pattern, by S. G. Chapman, is the shorter and simpler of the two, and is as follows:'

Cast on fourteen stitches.

1st row : Two plain, over, narrow, 1 plain, over, narrow, 7 plain.

2d row : 8 plain, over, narrow, 1 plain, over, narrow, 1 plain.

Repeat these two rows. The first eight stitches are for the heading; the six plain are to be dropped from the needle when the fringe is of the required length. The remaining eight to be cast off. The six dropped are to be unravelled for the fringe.

ANOTHER PATTERN.

The second pattern is by Mrs. C. S. Hastings, and forms a very handsome border and fringe well adapted for counterpanes, etc.

Cast on 24 stitches.

1st row : Slip 1, knit 1, over, purl 2 together, 1 plain, over and purl 2 together four times, 7 plain ; take two lengths of the fringe, double them in the middle, put the doubled part over the left needle, close to the next loop, and knit this loop and the fringe together, as if you were narrowing ; next knit 2 plain, bring the fringe in front, between these two stitches and the last, and knit this last stitch plain. The last four stitches in every odd row are knitted with the fringe in the same way all through the border. The "over" before a purl stitch, remember, is made by bringing the wool forward and then turning it once around the right needle.

2d row: Slip 1, knit plain the rest, except the last 4 stitches ; then over, purl 2 together, 2 plain.

3d row: Slip 1, knit 1, over, purl 2 together, 2 plain, over and purl 2 together four times, 6 plain ; insert fringe as before in the last four stitches.

4th row : Same as second.

5th row : Slip 1, knit 1, over, purl 2 together, 3 plain, over and purl 2 together four times, 5 plain ; insert fringe, etc.

6th row : Same as second.

7th row : Slip 1, knit 1, over, purl 2 together, 4 plain, over and purl 2 together four times, 4 plain ; insert fringe.

8th row : Same as second.

9th row : Slip 1, knit 1, over, purl 2 together, 5 plain, over and purl 2 together four times, 3 plain ; insert fringe.

10th row : Same as second.

11th row : Slip 1, knit 1, over, purl 2 together r 6 plain, over and purl 2 together four times, 2 plain; insert fringe.

12th row : Same as second.

13th row: Slip 1, knit 1, over, purl 2 together, 7 plain, over and purl 2 together four times, 1 plain ; insert fringe.

14th row : Same as second.

Repeat from the first row.

The fringe may be made of uniform length by winding the cotton or wool around a book, and cutting it where the hook opens. The border has a little open edging running along the top, with four rows of holes running slantingly downwards and forming a kind of long open-work diamond.

The Knitting Department would suggest a modification of this pattern, which some readers will probably find a pretty variation. Instead of repeating from the first after the fourteenth row, work backwards, thus :

15th row : Same as the eleventh.

16th and all even rows same as second.

17th row : Same as the ninth.

19th row: Same as the seventh.

21st row : Same as the fifth.

23d row: Same as the third.

On the twenty-fifth row repeat from the first. The original pattern consists of 14 rows, the modified one here suggested of 24 rows. The edging at the top and the fringe at the bottom are the same in both; but while the open-work in the middle forms an elongated diamond in the first pattern, it consists of a vandyke or zig-zag of four rows of holes in the second.

A COUNTERPANE OR SPREAD.

Cast on 81 stitches.

Knit 17, thread over, knit 4, slip 1, narrow, pass slip stitch over this one, knit 4, over, knit 1, over, knit 4, slip 1, narrow, pass slip stitch over, knit 4, over, knit 1, over, knit 4, slip 1, narrow, pass slip stitch over, knit 4, over, knit 1, over, knit 4, slip 1, narrow, pass slipped stitch over, knit 4, over, knit 17.

2nd row : Knit 4, purl 8, knit 4, purl until only 16 are left on left hand needle, knit 4, purl 8, knit 4.

Repeat these two rows until there are six of those open spaces, one above the other, made by the thread passed over the needle.

The right side of your work is now toward you—knit 4, take a hair-pin about the size of your needles, as it will not drop out like a needle, and slip the next 4 on to this and turn it over *back* of your needles while you knit the next 4; then take the hair-pin, pass the stitches along on the pin so that you knit the one first slipped from the needle first, knit 5. Now purl until 17 are on the left hand needle, knit 5, slip the next 4 off and bring the pin *toward* you or in front of your needles, knit the next 4, then from the hair-pin—*always* being careful to knit the first stitch taken from the needle first—knit 4.

Next : Knit 4, purl 8, knit 4, purl 1, knit all but 17, purl 1, knit 4, purl 8, knit 4.

Next: Knit 17; purl all except 17; knit 17.

Next: Knit 4, purl 8, knit 4, purl 1; knit all but 17; purl 1, knit 4, purl 8, knit 4.

Commence again at the beginning and repeat until the strip is as long as desired. Where sheet shams are used it need not be as long unless preferred. No. 10, 3 thread Dexter cotton was recommended to me and what I used; rather coarse needles necessary.

A nice trimming for bed linen is made thus:

Cast on 18 stitches. Knit 1st row across plain.

2d row: Seam (or purl) 15, leaving 4 on left-hand needle, not knitting them.

3d row: Slip 1, knit 9, knit 2 together (or narrow), thread over needle twice, knit 2.

4th row: Seam 14, making one stitch of the 2 loops.

5th row: Slip 1 stitch, knit 13. Next knit all the 18 stitches. This makes one quilling.

6th row: Knit 4, thread forward and seam 14.

7th row: Knit 1, narrow, thread over twice, knit 11.

8th row: Slip 1, seam 13, the 2 loops as 1 stitch.

9th row: Knit the whole 18. Repeat from 1st.

I send a sample after these directions. It can be made any width by increasing or diminishing the number of stitches. A lady here is knitting some for pillow shams, wider and of linen thread. For the neck of children's dresses it is pretty, as it needs no fluting, no ironing and but very little starch. It can be put to a multiplicity of uses, as one can readily see.　　　　P. M. Titus.

DEEP CROCHET LACE.

Mrs. C. Peterson kindly sends the following directions for making this lace:

Foundation chain of 17 stitches.

First row: 1 DC in 6th stitch from last, 3ch, 3 DC in 9th stitch; 3ch, 3 DC in same (9th) stitch,

fasten down to next stitch of chain, 3 chain, 3 DC in 15th stitch. 3ch, 3 DC in same stitch, fasten to the chain; 3ch, 3 DC in 17th stitch, 3ch, 3 DC in same stitch; fasten.

Second row: 3ch, 3 DC in loop made by the 3ch worked between the last 3 DC in preceding row, 3ch, 3 DC in same loop, 3ch, 3 DC in next loop; 3ch, 3 DC in same loop, 3ch, 3 DC in next or 3rd loop, 3ch, 3 DC in same loop; fasten, work 6ch, fasten to loop in the last row but one.

Third row: * 3ch, 1 DC, repeat from * 5 times, putting all the DC's in same large loop; then 3ch, 3 DC in next loop, 3ch, 3 DC in same loop; 3ch, 3

DC in second loop, 3ch, 3 DC in same loop, fasten; 3ch, 3 DC in 3rd and last loop, 3ch, 3 DC in same loop.

Fourth row: 3ch, 3 DC in first loop, 3ch, 3 DC in same; 3ch, 3 DC in second loop, 3ch, 3 DC in same; 3ch, 3 DC in 3rd loop, 3ch, 3 DC in same; 3ch, fasten over 1st. DC in large loop; repeat over every DC in scallop: fasten last 3ch to little scallop in last large scallop.

Fifth row: Into every loop made on the scallop in last row put 1 SC, 3 DC, 1 SC; fasten the little scallop down snugly, as much of the beauty of the work depends on their finish; then when you arrive at the body of the work begin again from the first row.

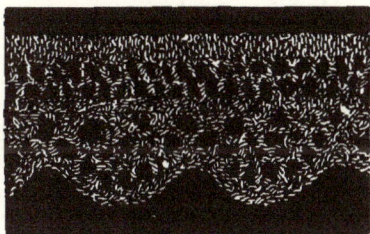

KNITTED LACE.

The pattern represented above looks best when worked in fine materials with correspondingly fine needles.

Cast on 8 stitches and work back plain.

First row: Over, narrow (or knit 2 together) 3 plain, over, narrow, 1 plain. (The "over" is made at the beginning of a row by simply placing the right needle under the thread.)

Second row: Slip 1, 2 plain, over, narrow, 1 plain, over, 2 plain.

Third row: Over, narrow, 4 plain, over, narrow, 1 plain.

Fourth row: Slip 1, 2 plain, over, narrow, 2 plain, over, 2 plain.

Fifth row: Over, narrow, 2 plain, over, narrow, 1 plain, over, narrow, 1 plain.

Sixth row: Slip 1, 2 plain, over, narrow, in next loop, which is the "over" of the previous row, knit 1 and purl 1, that is, after drawing the thread through in knitting 1 and before slipping the loop off the left needle, bring the thread forward and purl or seam a stitch in the same loop. Then slip it off, and finish the row thus—narrow, over, 2 plain.

Seventh row: Over, narrow, 6 plain, over, narrow, 1 plain.

Eighth row: Slip 1, 2 plain, over, narrow, 2 plain, over, 1 plain, over, narrow, 1 plain.

Ninth row: Over, narrow, 2 plain, in next loop knit 1 and purl 1 (as in sixth row), narrow, 2 plain, over, narrow, 1 plain.

Tenth row: Slip 1, 2 plain, over, narrow, 2 plain, narrow, over, narrow, 1 plain.

Eleventh row: Over, narrow, 1 plain, narrow, over, narrow, 1 plain, over, narrow, 1 plain.

Twelfth row: Slip 1, 2 plain, over, narrow, in next loop knit 1 and purl 1, then 1 plain, over, narrow, 1 plain

Thirteenth row: Over, narrow, 1 plain, narrow twice, 1 plain, over, narrow, 1 plain.

Fourteenth row: Slip 1, 2 plain, over, narrow, 1 plain, over, narrow, 1 plain.

Fifteenth row: Over, narrow, 1 plain, narrow, 1 plain, over, narrow, 1 plain.

Sixteenth row: Slip 1, 2 plain, over, narrow, over, narrow, 1 plain.

Repeat from first row. The slip stitch should be done as in purling. Place the needle under the thread, slip the stitch and put the thread back ready for the knitted stitches.

PANSY MATS.

These pretty table mats are easily worked, and will bring with them such pleasant memories of Spring flowers that many readers will try to find a dainty corner for them. For a pair of small mats which shall closely imitate natural colors, take two ounces of dark green single zephyr wool, an ounce each of bright canary yellow and shaded purple, and a medium-sized hook, say about the size of a number 11 or 12 knitting needle.

First round: With the green make a little ring about half the size of a silver five-cent piece, by twisting the loose end of the wool around a loop. Put the hook under the ring from the inside, catch the wool and make three chain. This represents the first treble. Next work in the ring as many trebles as it will hold, and join to top of the 3 ch. with a SC.

Second round: 2 trebles in every stitch.

Third round: * 1 treble in the first, 2 trebles in the next; repeat from * all round.

Fourth round: * 1 treble each in the 1st and 2d, 2 trebles in the 3d stitch; repeat from * all round.

Fifth round: * 1 treble each in the first 3 stitches, 2 trebles in the 4th; repeat from *.

The main point in these rounds is to see that the work lies perfectly flat, and the above instructions may need a little modification, according to the judgment of the worker. Thus in the fourth round it may be found best to increase only every third and fourth stitch alternately, instead of every third, and in the fifth round to increase every fourth and fifth stitch alternately, instead of every fourth.

Sixth row: Now join on the canary wool, and work a row of DC, increasing about every 8th stitch all round.

Seventh round: Fasten on the green again and work a round of trebles, increasing (that is, working two stitches in one loop) about every 6th stitch.

Eighth round: Work (also in green) a round of DC, increasing about every 10th stitch.

Ninth round: Join on the canary and work three trebles into every loop.

Tenth round: With the purple work as follows:

* Three trebles into the first stitch, 1 DC into the next, 1 DC into the third; repeat from * all round.

This completes the mat. The pansies around it can be arranged to suit the taste of the worker, and if desired various points may be stitched together with a little of the purple wool.

Another variety of the pansy mat has been kindly sent in by A. P. S. A., who thus describes it:

Crochet with white single zephyr wool four or five chain stitches. Join these in a circle and crochet round and round in DC till you have increased to 84 stitches, making a circle about six inches in diameter, and taking care, by suitable increasings, to keep it as flat as possible. The next row is worked with very dark green single zephyr in SC all round, crocheting between instead of in each stitch. The next row is done in lemon-colored single zephyr, working between every green stitch 4 DC stitches. The last row is worked in shaded purple single zephyr, getting that which has the darkest shades. Begin this row with 1 chain stitch, then 6 DC stitches between the groups of 4 DC's in the preceding row, then 1 chain and catch over in the middle of each yellow group. Repeat in this way all round.

When finished, the border of the mat should look like a full ruffle. Now take five of the purple shells, and join the first and fifth lightly underneath. Then skip two shells; take five more and proceed as before. This has the effect of a circle of pansies laid closely together.

To make a larger mat, add seven stitches on the last white row for each additional pansy.

AFGHANS—TWO PATTERNS.

Those who abide in country houses or by the sea-shore in Summer are always in need of an afghan for light covering during afternoon naps on wicker lounges or hammocks, or during picnic excursions. The making of them is pleasant work for these early Spring days, and we gladly give, in addition to those already presented, these two patterns, sent by R. R., Northampton, Mass. She writes: " Wishing to show my appreciation of the Knitting Column in your paper —which, although not a subscriber, I am fortunate enough to see—I send herewith directions for a 'Hit-or-Miss Afghan,' which is made as follows:

HIT OR MISS AFGHAN.

" Tie together odds and ends of worsteds, such as every one has in the house. Make a chain half as long again as the afghan will be when done, for the crocheting takes up. Crochet 13 rows lengthwise in fan stitch.

" For the 14th row take black wool; for the 15th row yellow.

" Then make another row of black; then 13 rows of some solid color—dark red, for instance. Next to the red put a row of black, then a row of yellow, then another of black, then 13 of 'hit-or-miss,' and so on till your afghan is of the desired size.

" I use Germantown yarn for the black and for the

solid color. It is cheaper and firmer than Berlin wool."

ROMAN AFGHAN.

I have not seen directions for a Roman Afghan in the column, and send the following:

The stripes are arranged thus: Black, Roman, black, Roman, and black—five in all. There are fifty stitches in each stripe, 275 ribs in length. Crochet stripes together with four stitches of black, four of white, and four of yellow. Germantown yarn. Needles about No. 8. Plain knitting.

The Roman stripe is worked thus: One double row or rib of white, 1 of blue, 1 of pink, 1 of blue, 1 of yellow, 1 of pink, 1 of white, 12 blue.

One rib of white, 1 of blue, 1 of pink, 1 of blue, 1 of yellow, 1 of pink, 1 of white, 12 black.

One rib white, 1 pink, 1 blue, 1 yellow, 1 of white, 1 of pink, 1 of blue, 10 white.

One rib blue, 1 white, 1 pink, 1 blue, 1 of yellow,

1 pink, 1 white, 10 pink. Repeat this to end of stripe. Mix the thread of the yellow with three of black in the fringe on the ends of the Afghan. The first stitch is knit by putting forward thread and taking it up as in seaming. Crochet on the edges, as between the stripes.

This is a very handsome afghan. I find that the "Columbia" Germantown is the best.

BABY'S BOOT.

Materials—White Andalusian wool, Needles—No. 10. Cast on 27 stitches, knit one row plain, purl 1 row, knit 11 rows, increasing on the 3d stitch of every row. There should now be 38 stitches on the needle. Purl 1 row, knit 11 rows, decreasing by knitting 2d and 3d stitches together in every row. There should now be 27 stitches. Purl 1 row, increasing on the 3d stitch; cast on 10 stitches for heel. There should now be 38 stitches. Knit 0 rows, purl 1 row and knit 5 rows, increasing

at the toe end only. There will now be 43 stitches. Knit 25 stitches, leaving 20 stitches on another needle, and knit backward and forward for front of foot as follows: 1st row, Knit 25.—2d row. Purl 25.—3d row. Knit 1, 2 together 12 times. —4th row. Knit 1, take up 1, same to end. These 4 rows form the pattern, and must be repeated 4 times more, making in all 20 rows for front of foot; make 20 stitches for side of foot. Knit 5 rows, purl 1 row, knit 7 rows, decreasing at the toe end only, cast off.

For leg—Take up the 20 stitches on the side knitting, also 11 for front, then knit the 20 left on spare needle, knit 1 row, purl 1 row, 1 row of holes by putting wool twice round needle and knitting 2 together, purl 1 row, then 5 patterns same as front of foot—21st row. Knit 3, purl 3, knit 3, purl 3 to end of row.—22d and 23d like 21st.—24th row. Purl 3, knit 3, purl 3, knit 3 to end.—25th and 26th like 24th.—27th, 28th and 29th like 21st. —30th row. Plain. Repeat as 30th 5 times more. Cast off on wrong side.

SHELL-EDGED LACES.

Two contributors have kindly sent in patterns of shell-edged laces, which will prove useful varieties to many knitters. The former is by L. E. W., and the latter by Mrs. A. M. C.

FIRST PATTERN.

Cast on 15 stitches, knit across plain.

1st row: Slip 1, knit 1, over, narrow, over, narrow, over 2, narrow, knit 0, over 2, purl 1. (In over 2 before a purl stitch bring thread forward and throw round needle twice.)

2d row: Over, purl 2 together, drop 1, knit 8, purl 1, knit 0.

3d row: Slip 1, knit 1, over, narrow, over, narrow, knit 9, over 2, purl 2 together.

4th row: Over, purl 2 together, drop 1, knit 15.

("Over" at the beginning of a row before a purl stitch, is made by putting needle under thread and throwing the thread once around the needle.)

5th row: Slip 1, knit 1, over, narrow, over, narrow, over 2, narrow, over 2, narrow, knit 5, over 2, purl 2 together.

6th row: Over, purl 2 together, drop 1, knit 7, purl 1, knit 2, purl 1, knit 6.

7th row: Slip 1, knit 1, over, narrow, over, narrow, knit 11, over 2, purl 2 together.

8th row: Over, purl 2 together, drop 1, knit 17.

9th row: Slip 1, knit 1, over, narrow, over, narrow, over 2, narrow, over 2, narrow, over 2, narrow, knit 5, over 2, purl 2 together.

10th row: Over, purl 2 together, drop 1, knit 7, purl 1, knit 2, purl 1, knit 2, purl 1, knit 6.

11th row: Slip 1, knit 1, over, narrow, over, narrow, knit 14, over 2, purl 2 together.

12th row: Over, purl 2 together, drop 1, knit 6, with the point of the left needle slip 7 off over the last one knit; knit 14.

Repeat from 1st row.

SECOND PATTERN.

Cast on 20 stitches.

1st row: 3 plain, over twice and seam or purl 2 together (this is what was called "beading" in knitting thirty-five or forty years ago); 3 plain, over twice and narrow (by knitting 2 together); rest plain. In "over twice" before a purl stitch, bring thread forward and then put twice around the needle.

2d row: 3 plain, over twice, narrow (or knit 2 together), 7 plain, 1 purl, 3 plain, over twice, purl 2 together, drop the next loop (the second of the "over twice"), 3 plain.

3d row: 3 plain, over twice, purl 2 together, drop 1, 3 plain (these 0 stitches form the upper part of the lace and are worked always alike at the beginning of every odd row and at the end of every even row; hereafter they will be called the "border"); 10 plain, drop the next, 3 plain.

4th row: 13 plain; border.

5th row: Border; over twice, narrow, 1 plain, over twice, narrow, rest plain.

6th row: 3 plain, over twice, narrow, 5 plain, 1 purl, 3 plain, 1 purl; border.

7th row: Border; 12 plain, drop the next, 3 plain.

8th row: 15 plain; border.

9th row: Border; over twice, narrow, 1 plain, over twice, narrow, 10 plain.

10th row: 3 plain, over twice, narrow, 7 plain, 1 purl, 3 plain, 1 purl; border.

11th row: Border; 14 plain, drop 1, 3 plain.

12th row: 17 plain; border.

13th row: Border; over twice, narrow, 1 plain, over twice, narrow, 1 plain, over twice, narrow, rest plain.

14th row: 3 plain, over twice, narrow, 6 plain, 1 purl, 3 plain, 1 purl, 3 plain, 1 purl; border.

15th row: Border; 17 plain, drop 1, 3 plain.

16th row: 9 plain, with the point of the left needle t' row the 8th over the 9th and then succes-

sively the first 7, leaving only one loop (the 9th) on the right needle; then 11 plain; border.

Repeat from 1st row, remembering to drop always in the "border" the long loop after the purl 2 together.

A HANDSOME INSERTION (KNITTING).

"A New Contributor" will please accept THE TRIBUNE's thanks for the following:

Having received great pleasure from your knitting column and been successful in knitting the patterns which I have attempted, I will inclose a sample of insertion—with directions for knitting—which will match the "Knitted Point" issued in "The Woman's Extra" No. 59:

Cast on 22 stitches.

1st row: Knit 3, * thread before needle as in purling, narrow, repeat 3 times from *, knit 5, purl 1, knit 1, purl 1, knit 3.

2d row: Knit 3, * thread before needle, narrow, repeat once from *, knit 0, purl 1, knit 1, purl 1, knit 3.

3d row: Knit 3, * thread before needle, narrow, repeat once from *, knit 1, * thread before needle, narrow, repeat once from *, knit 4, purl 1, knit 1, purl 1, knit 3.

4th row: Same as 2d row.

5th row: Knit 3, * thread before needle, narrow, repeat once from *, knit 2, * thread before needle, narrow, repeat once from *, knit 3, purl 1, knit 1, purl 1, knit 3.

6th row: Same as 2d row.

7th row: Knit 3, * thread before needle, narrow, repeat once from *, knit 3, * thread before needle, narrow, repeat once from *, knit 2, purl 1, knit 1, purl 1, knit 3.

8th row: Same as 2nd row.

9th row: Knit 3, * thread before needle, narrow, repeat once from , knit 4, * thread before needle, narrow, repeat from *, knit 1, purl 1, knit 1, purl 1, knit 3.

10th row: Same as 2d row.

11th row: Knit 3, thread before needle, narrow, repeat once from *, knit 5, * thread before needle, narrow, repeat once from *, purl 1, knit 1, purl 1, knit 3.

PATTERN FOR A SCRAP BAG.

Miss N. A. P. very obligingly responds to a request for a scrap-bag pattern. With knitting-cotton No. 18 and a fine Afghan crochet-hook make a chain of 30 stitches; then, in Afghan or "tricotée" stitch, work from foundation a strip about two fingers long. Then begin to narrow on each edge by skipping a stitch as you take up a needle full. Continue this until you have narrowed down to one stitch. Make three strips just alike, then with scarlet wool (stocking yarn is good as any) work any device you please on each strip—initials, date or flowers. Then crochet all around each strip in red yarn, with 5 chain fastened to strip, with 1 SC at equal distances apart. Leave the straight end plain.

Now with the white cotton crochet the whole together, leaving the straight end for the top. Sew in a strip of white bonnet-wire and finish around the top with shellwork in the red. Suspend with three cords and a couple of tassels; also sew at the points where the three sections are joined a couple of tassels, and short loops to hang the tassels by. This is to be hung on or near the sewing-machine. It can be made of red trimmed with white if desired. Our friend adds: "I am greatly interested in the Knitting Column, and as I have been an invalid for nearly two years and most of that time has been spent in my bed, I have a chance to try most of the stitches that I did not know already. I have knit three pairs of those little socks like the pattern in THE TRIBUNE of January 8, and every one who sees them wants a pair. All say 'How lovely!' and I have four or five pairs more to knit yet. If my pattern is of any use in the Knitting Column I may send other directions, as I feel under obligations for benefits received from that department of THE TRIBUNE." THE TRIBUNE is peculiarly glad to be of service and comfort to sufferers like N. A. P. It cordially thanks her both for the clear directions she sends and for her promise of other patterns.

RICE-STITCH.

This fancy stitch in crochet is easily learned, and is pretty for shawls, clouds, etc. Make a chain of

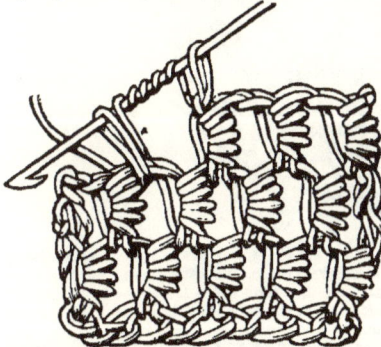

any length you wish. Wind your thread five times around the needle—put the needle through the 2d loop of the foundation chain—pass the needle under the thread, draw the thread through the loop, and then draw the thread through all the loops upon the needle. This makes a group of threads like grains of rice. Make a chain stitch before proceeding to make the next group. In the next row the groups are to be placed in the chain stitch of the preceding row, as shown in the cut.

This pattern is easily understood but it will take a good deal of practice before it can be done quickly. Another pattern which admits of more rapid manipulation is worked thus:

Make a foundation chain. Wind the thread around the needle, put the needle through the 2d loop of the chain, pass the needle under the thread, draw it through the loop of the chain only; repeat this movement twice more through the same loop. There will now be 7 threads or loops on the needle; pass the needle under the thread, draw it through 6 of the 7 loops, pass the needle under the thread, draw it through the 2 loops left on the needle. This makes a group. Make a chain stitch before making another group; and in the next row put the groups in the chain stitches of the preceding row.

INFANT'S SHIRT.

M. F. B., Frederick, Md., is herewith offered the cordial thanks of this department, both for her pleasant letter and the "Infant's Shirt" pattern accompanying it. She says: "The knitting column has been such a pleasure to me, that I wish to express my grateful appreciation of it. I have many times thought I would send it some help, but I am a writer, and so busy, it is hard to take time, and it is not possible to do such a thing to any purpose, unless it is written out with great care and clearness to make it intelligible to all. However, when I saw that a correspondent had asked for a rule for baby's shirts, I felt that I must send mine, if everything stood still, for I owe it to you after all the nice things you have helped me to. I have an excellent baby-sock pattern, and will try and send that if you wish. I hope this will please C. M. M., and am very gratefully your delighted reader." THE TRIBUNE will be pleased to publish the sock pattern. The directions for the "Infant's Shirt," are as follows:

Cast on 73 stitches. It should be understood that when stitches are set up they must be knitted once across plain and very loose in order to make a good edge, and first stitches are always slipped without knitting for the same reason.

1st row: Slip 1st, slip 2d, knit 1 plain and bind (or cast) 2d over it, over, 1 plain, over. 1 plain, over, 1 plain, over, 1 plain, over, 1 plain, over, 1 plain, over, 1 plain, narrow (or knit 2 together), purl 1; repeat from "slip 2d" to the end of the row.

2d row: Slip 1st, purl 16, knit 1 plain, purl 16, knit 1 plain; repeat to end of row.

3d row: Slip 1st, slip 2d, knit 3d plain and bind 2d over it, knit 12 plain, narrow, purl 1; repeat from "slip 2d" to end of row.

4th row: Slip 1st, purl 14, knit 1 plain, purl 14, knit 1 plain; repeat to end of row.

5th row: Slip 1st, slip 2d, knit 3d plain and bind 2d over 3d, knit 10 plain, narrow, purl 1, and repeat as in 3d and 1st rows to the end.

6th row: Slip 1st, purl 10, purl 2 together, knit 1 plain, purl 10, purl 2 together, knit 1 plain. and repeat to the end of row.

This makes the whole pattern, and when done should leave the 73 stitches begun with. It is to be repeated six times, which makes the bottom part of the shirt body. Above this it should be simply ribbed by knitting 2 plain and 2 purl, 2 plain and 2 purl back and forth till it is as long as desired; 9 inches is about right. Then knit a row of holes across the top for the cord which draws the neck, and cast off. Seventy stitches are enough for the ribbed part, and the three extra stitches may be disposed of by binding them off gradually, anywhere throughout the 1st row of the ribbed part. They must not be done all together or it would show. Two pieces knit like the above, and sewed together with the wool (which should be 3-threaded Saxony yarn), make the body, and these side seams are to be left open 4½ inches from the top, for the sleeve. Any pretty lace pattern of 13 to 15 stitches will answer for this. I have always used the one on p. 4 of the "Woman's Extra" No. 59, and this is how you must use it : Having made 12 points knit about 14 or 15 rows plain, which will

make a little square piece on the end. This is for a gusset and is to be sewed to the other end like any gusset cut on a chemise sleeve. Then sew it into the place left in the side seam with the point set in where the seam was left open.

The holes round the top of the body are made in this way, beginning on the right side, of course: Slip 1, over, narrow, 1 plain, over, narrow, 1 plain, over, to end of row. Knit back all plain, then cast off.

This makes the prettiest infants' shirt I have ever seen. If they are required to be high in the neck it can be done by narrowing off gradually (at what would be the top, otherwise) to fit the shoulder; probably eight stitches on each side would be enough. An open place must be left in one breadth for the neck. This is easily done by dividing the number of stitches by 2, and knitting the two halves up separately. This leaves the little slit for the front. They are very durable, and if laundried

properly will last a long time. The baby always outgrows them, in fact, and they will not shrink much unless they are badly rinsed and soapsuds left in them. In fact that is what ruins all sorts of woollen goods, which would last as long as anything else otherwise.

DAISY PATTERN.

This is a very useful pattern, as it can be employed in making a great variety of things—counterpanes, convrettes for chairs, sofas and bureaus, mats, pincushions and lace. It can be worked in cotton, silk or wool.

Each circle is made separately and joined to the others, as the last row is crocheted. Begin in the centre; make 8 chain; insert the needle in the first

stitch of the chain, and make * a long treble stitch ; then make 3 chain. Repeat 4 times from *, always inserting the needle in the 1st chain stitch ; join the last chain to the 5th of the 1st 8 chain to close the round.

2d round: Work 1 DC ; * 9 chain, turn, work an SC stitch in each of the 9 chain ; work round the stem thus made in DC, working 3 stitches in 1 to turn at the point ; miss 1 stitch of preceding row, work 2 DC ; this makes a petal ; repeat from * 5 times more, making 6 petals in all. A glance at the cut will help to explain this.

3d round: Work at the back of the last row, behind the petals ; make 1 petal between each petal in the last row, 1 DC at the back of each (which fastens the petal into its looped shape) and cut the cotton at the end of the round.

4th row : Work 2 DC at the point of each of the 12 petals ; 5 chain between each petal.

5th round : Work 2 treble at the point of each petal and between each petal, connecting each group of 2 treble by a 5 chain.

6th and last round: Work 1 DC in the centre of the 1st 5 chain, * 5 chain, 1 treble in the centre of the next 5 chain, 5 chain, 1 SC in the top of the treble stitch, 6 chain, 1 SC in the same place, 5 chain, a third SC in the same place, 5 chain; repeat from * to the end of the round. This forms the open clover leaves surrounding each circle; there should be 12 of these leaves in the round.

In making a spread, couvrette, etc., join the circles together as shown in cut, in working the last round. Use whatever number of circles you please.

TABLE MATS.

Make a chain of 25 stitches.

DC. all around to the beginning and turn the work. There is one stitch upon the hook; put the hook back through the last loop through which the cotton was drawn, put the cotton over the hook and

draw it through that loop alone; then put the cotton over the hook and draw through the two loops upon the hook—DC. the row of loops on the back side of the mat to the end.

Crochet twice in each of three adjoining loops at the end—DC. to the other end. Crochet twice in two adjoining loops at that end, bringing the ends of the first row around the mat together.

Bring the cotton in front of the hook which has upon it one loop, put the hook through a loop at the end of this row where it commenced, and draw the cotton through the two loops upon the hook joining the row.

Turn the work over, put the hook back through the last loop that the cotton was drawn through, put the cotton over the hook, draw through that loop alone, put the cotton over the hook and draw through the two loops.

Crochet twice in the first loop of each of the two loops that had two stitches put in them.

Proceed down the side to the other end—Crochet twice in the first of each of the three loops that had two stitches put in them, then go on to the begin-

ning of the row, join and turn over the mat as before.

Continue until the mat is of sufficient size.

For the border pass one loop and make in the second five TC. stitches. Pass one loop and fasten down by DC. in the next, and so on around the mat.

The length of the chain in the middle of course determines the size of the mat. For coffee and tea pots make a chain of six, and fasten together. Crochet twice in every stitch to start the six points for widening.

The cotton suitable is Dexter's No. 6 four threads. A hook small enough to make it very compact should be used. The stitches to be crocheted all the time are upon the back of the mat.

The mat, it will be seen, is worked in ribbed (DC) crochet, the hook being placed in the outside half of each loop, and the work turned at the end of each round. The increasings are of course, to turn the corners, and the rounds are completed by an SC. before turning back.

NARROW KNITTED LACE.

Cast on 9 stitches.

1st row: Knit 3, narrow, over, narrow, over, knit 1, over, knit 1.

2d row: Knit 1, purl 1, knit 1, purl 1, knit 1, purl 1, knit 4.

3d row: Knit 2, narrow, over, narrow, over, knit 3, over, knit 1.

4th row: Knit 1, purl 1, knit 3, purl 1, knit 1, purl 1, knit 3.

5th row: Knit 1, narrow, over, narrow, over, knit 5, over, knit 1.

6th row: Knit 1, purl 1, knit 5, purl 1, knit 1, purl 1, knit 2.

7th row: Knit 3, over, narrow, over, narrow, knit 1, narrow, over, narrow.

8th row: Knit 1, purl 1, knit 3, purl 1, knit 1, purl 1, knit 3.

9th row: Knit 4, over, narrow, over, knit 3 together, over, narrow.

10th row: Knit 1, purl 1, knit 1, purl 1, knit 1, purl 1, knit 4.

11th row: Knit 5, over, knit 3 together, over narrow.

12th row: Knit 1, purl 1, knit 1, purl 1, knit 5.

Repeat from beginning.

KNITTED PURSES.

These may either be knitted round with five needles, or in a flat piece with two needles, and afterward sewn up. The latter is perhaps the easier way. The ends of the purse are usually made close and compact with an open pattern in the centre, but often some simple fancy pattern is used throughout, and beads are frequent ornamental additions.

With fine purse silk and needles—say 18 to 20—130 or 140 stitches will not be too many. With coarser silk and No. 16 to 18 needles, 90 to 100 stitches will be enough. For a plain strong purse with 90 stitches and No. 17 needles, proceed as follows:

1st row: 30 stitches plain; the next 30, * over and knit 2 together; repeat from *; the last 30 plain.

2d row: plain throughout. Repeat these two rows till the purse is wide enough. Then sew up, leaving a slit where the open work is to put in the money. Draw up the two ends and add rings and tassels.

If an open work pattern is required throughout one of these may be adopted:

1. 1st row: Knit 2 together, make 1, knit 1; repeat.

2d row: plain.

Repeat these two rows.

2. 1st row: Over, knit 3, and draw the first of the 3 over the other two; repeat.

2d row: plain.

Repeat these two rows.

By changing the silk every few rows, the purse will be knit in narrow stripes. All knitted purses are improved by being damped and then stretched out till dry. These directions are given in response to many requests.

MATS.

Knitting-needles number 14; red Saxony yarn and Dexter cotton number 12. Cast on 22 stitches.

1st row: Knit 15, make 1, purl 2 together, knit 1, make 2, knit 2 together, make 2, knit 2 together.

2d row: Knit 2, purl 1, knit 2, purl 1, knit 1, make 1, purl 2 together, knit 3.

3d row: Slip 1, knit 2, make 1, purl 2 together, knit 3, make 2, knit 2 together, make 2, knit 2 together.

4th row: Knit 2, purl 1, knit 2, purl 1, knit 3, make 1, purl 2 together, knit six.

5th row: Slip 1, knit 5, make 1, purl 2 together, knit 5, make 2, knit 2 together, make 2, knit 2 together.

6th row: Knit 2, purl 1, knit 2, purl 1, knit 5, make 1, purl 2 together, knit 9.

7th row: Slip 1, knit 8, make 1, purl 2 together, knit 7, make 2, knit 2 together, make 3, knit 2 together.

8th row: Knit 2, purl 1, knit 2, purl 1, knit 7, make 1, purl 2 together, knit 12.

9th row: Slip 1, knit 11, make 1, purl 2 together, knit plain to end of row.

10th row: Cast off until there are only 21 stitches left on the left-hand needle. Knit 4, make 1, purl 2 together, knit 15. These ten rows complete a pattern and are repeated twenty-four times. Then sew together and draw up, to lie smooth, the hole in the centre of the mat. Begin with the white cotton and join yarn for second point; do not break off the cotton but carry it around, as also the yarn. Always slip the first stitch in the odd rows, and al-

ways knit 3 more than on the previous row, in knitting the even rows. M. A. L. adds: "The mats may be made larger by casting on 30 stitches and knitting 21 before 'make 1 and purl 2 together.' Then knit 3 instead of 1 before ' make 2 and knit 2 together.' The result will be six eyelets on the edge instead of four.

INFANT'S SACQUE IN STAR STITCH.

Material: One skein white Shetland wool and one of blue.

Begin at the bottom, making a chain of 182 stitches, crochet 10 times across, keeping the edges straight. 11th row: Narrow in the centre of the back, then work 8 times across, narrowing in the centre of the back each time.

To make the arm-hole, crochet 10 stars; break your wool; omit one and proceed to the centre of the back, narrow one when within 11 stars of the other edge; break the wool and omit one star as on the other side; go 7 times across after this manner and you have a slot for the sleeve. Crochet across four times, narrowing on each shoulder and in the centre of the back.

For sleeve, set up a chain of 54 stitches; crochet round and round, not breaking the wool until you reach the top of the sleeve; 18 times round will be sufficient; crochet nearly round, omitting two stars; break the wool; crochet three times across, omitting one star at the beginning and dropping one at the end of each row; this will round up the top of the sleeve.

Finish with an edge of blue. The edging used on " Frock for Child," in a back number of THE TRIBUNE, is very pretty. A cord run in the neck, with balls of blue and white to be tied at the back, completes the sacque. This will be sufficiently large for a child from nine to twelve months old.

SHELL FOR KNITTED COUNTERPANE.

With No. 8 Dexter cotton and medium-sized steel needles cast on 44 stitches. Knit 1st, 3d and 5th rows plain. 2d row: Knit 2 together, over; repeat this 21 times, then knit 2 together.

4th row: Knit 2 together and over, 21 times, knit 1.

6th row: Slip 1, knit 2, narrow, knit the rest plain.

7th row: Slip 1, knit 2, narrow, purl all but 4, knit these plain.

The 8th, 9th, 11th, 12th, 14th, 15th, 17th, 18th, 20th, 21st, 23d, 24th, 26th, 27th, 29th, 30th, 32d,

33d, 35th, 36th, 38th, 39th, 40th, 41st and 42d rows are all knit like the 6th row.

The 10th, 13th, 16th, 19th, 22d, 25th, 28th, 31st, 34th and 37th rows are all knit like the 7th row.

43d row : Slip 1, knit 2, narrow, knit 2.

44th row : Slip 1, knit 1, narrow, knit 1.

45th row : Slip 1, narrow, knit 1.

46th row : Slip 1, narrow, slip the first stitch over the last and draw the thread through.

In joining these shells place each narrowed point to the centre of the first row of another shell, and allow all the points to run downward, then one can easily see where the other shells join in, and sew together.

BABY'S KNITTED BOOT.

This pretty boot is knitted on two needles, No. 10, with Saxony yarn.

Cast on 50 stitches and knit plain one row.

2d row: Knit 3, and then alternately 2 plain and 2 purl through the row, finishing with 3 plain. Repeat this row twice.

5th row: Plain.

6th row: Purl.

7th row: Slip 1, and knit 2 together up to the last stitch, which is plain.

8th row: Slip 1, over and knit 1 to the end, when the 50 stitches will be again on the needle.

9th row: Plain.

10th row: Purl.

11th row: Like the 7th.

12th row: Same as the 8th.

13th row: Plain.

14th row: Purl.

15th row: Plain, followed by 9 rows of rib, 2 plain and 2 purl, always commencing and ending by 3 plain.

first row of decreasing being worked thus: Slip 1, knit 2 together, 10 plain, 2 together, 20 plain, 2 together, 10 plain, 2 together, 1 plain. After the plain separating row, the second decreasing row is worked thus: Slip 1, knit 2 together, continue plain.

For the lacey instep, separate 16 of the centre stitches and work them apart, as for a heel. After a plain row, turn the work and purl, then knit backwards and forwards on these 16 stitches the four lines of holes, working them as in 7th, 8th, 9th, and 10th rows, and cast off.

With the right hand needle pick up the stitches on one side, and cast on 11 extra ones. * Knit 14 rows plain, then begin to decrease for shaping the lower part of the foot. Each of the five following diminishing rows alternates with a plain one.—Slip 1, knit 2 together to the end.—Slip 1, knit 2 together twice, and continue plain till the 3 last

25th row: Plain.

26th row: Purl.

Now for the quadruple band of holes. Repeat for each stripe the 7th, 8th, 9th and 10th rows. Make 2 rows of decreasing, separated by a plain one, the stitches, 2 of which are knitted together and 1 plain.—Slip 1, knit 2 together twice, remainder plain, till the 5 last stitches worked off by knitting 2 together twice and 1 plain.—Slip 1, knit 2 together twice, finish by 2 together and 1 plain.—Slip 1, knit 2 together, remainder plain. Cast off.

Pick up the 11 extra stitches and knit plain, increasing at the beginning of each row till there are 18 stitches on the needles. Three plain rows.—From thence decrease in the same proportion until only 11 stitches are left. Raise all the remaining stitches on the opposite side of the instep, and repeat from *. Sew up the boot, and finish off with a ribbon runner and bows.

KNITTED LACE.

Cast on 10 stitches.

1st row: Knit 2, over twice, purl 2 together, knit 2, over twice, narrow, knit 8.

2d row: Over, narrow, over, narrow, knit 6, purl 1, knit 2, over twice, purl 2 together, knit 2.

3d row: Slip 1, knit 1, over twice, purl 2 together, knit 13.

4th row: Over, narrow, over, narrow, knit 9, over twice, purl 2 together, 2 plain.

5th row: Slip 1, knit 1, over twice, purl 2 together, knit 1, over twice, narrow, over twice, narrow, knit 7.

6th row: Over, narrow, over, narrow, 5 plain, purl 1, knit 2, purl 1, knit 2, over twice, purl 2 together, knit 2.

7th row: Slip 1, knit 1, over twice, purl 2 together, knit the rest plain.

8th row: Over, narrow, over, narrow, 11 plain, over twice, purl 2 together, knit 2.

9th row: Slip 1, knit 1, over twice, purl 2 together, knit 2, over twice, narrow three times, rest plain.

10th row: Over, narrow twice, 4 plain, purl 1, 2 plain, purl 1, 2 plain, purl 1, 2 plain, over twice, purl 2 together, 2 plain.

11th row: Slip 1, knit 1, over twice, purl 2 together, rest plain.

12th row: Over, narrow, over, narrow, 6 plain, bind off 6, 8 plain, over twice, purl 2 together, knit 2.

Repeat from the 1st row. This lace is very pretty knitted with linen thread instead of wool, as the loops on the edge stand out better and make the pattern more showy.

INFANT'S CROCHETED SOCKS.

Socks for the little ones are in such constant demand that plain directions for crocheting a simple, useful pattern will be acceptable to beginners.

With single zephyr of the desired color and a rather small hook make a chain long enough to go around baby's leg—probably thirty-five stitches, more or less. Join them together to form around, and work in DC., putting the hook through the underhalf of each stitch for about 15 rounds. This forms the leg.

Now, for the top part of the foot, take 13 stitches, crochet tricotée—that is, put in the hook as before, pull the wool through and leave the loop on the hook. Work these 13 stitches forward and backward in crochet tricotée for 10 rows—remembering that forward and backward make 1 row. On the next row narrow by drawing the wool through the first 3 vertical stitches on the right hand side of the piece, and again through the 3 stitches immediately before the last loop. Repeat these narrowings on the next row. There are now 5 stitches. Make a DC. in each. The top part of the foot is finished.

Next, work down the left side of this piece in DC., then around the stitches at the bottom of the leg, and afterward along the right of the foot and around the toe. In doing this the only part to be careful about is the left side of the foot. The hook here should be put under the last of the Afghan stitches down the side and through the stitch below. Work round and round the bottom of foot and leg in DC. for 6 or 7 rounds. Then turn the work inside out, place the two sides carefully together, put the hook through 7 stitches at the top end and draw the wool through the whole. Crochet in DC. the bottom edges of the foot together till only 7 stitches are left, put the hook through all of these, draw them together to match the toe end, fasten off, turn it inside out again, and the foot is finished.

Next fasten the wool on the top of the leg; make three chains, work two treble into the same hole, miss two stitches, and fasten with a DC. into the third stitch. Make two chain, work two trebles into the same hole as the DC.; miss two stitches and work a DC. on the third. Repeat this scallop all around the top of the leg.

The work is now complete with the exception of a little chain and tassels, or a narrow ribbon around the ankle. The pattern will hardly be called a handsome one, but it is easily made and understood.

Recapitulation: Cast on 35 stitches for top of leg; leg 15 rounds deep, top of foot 13 stitches wide, and ten rows to narrowings for the toe. Two rows of narrowings—8 stitches in all; toe, 5 stitches wide; depth of foot, 6 or 7 rounds. Finish with scallop on leg and ribbon round ankle.

BUTTONS.

Many crocheted worsted articles, especially those intended for children, are often ornamented by what are commonly known as "buttons." These are raised little balls, and are made in several ways according to the particular kind of crochet used. In hoods and sacques for little folks, worked in crochet tricotée or Afghan stitch, "buttons" are very commonly used.

To make them, first work a complete row of Afghan stitch in the ordinary way, forward and backward, and raise all the stitches for the second row. In working these off, first catch the wool and draw it through one stitch. Catch it again and draw it through two. Now make a chain of four stitches. This forms the first button. Catch the wool again, and draw it through two loops and repeat three times. Then make another chain of four stitches, and repeat this process to the end. The first "button," it will be noted, is made after the second stitch, and there are four stitches between each succeeding button.

In raising the next row pick up only the vertical

stitches as usual, and be careful that the hook is placed behind the buttons in raising the vertical stitch beyond each of them. Work back this row plain; that is, without buttons. Raise all the stitches once more, work off four and then make a button. Work off four more and make another button. Repeat this to the end. The buttons in this row fall midway between those of the first row—not directly over them. These two rows of buttons are repeated throughout the work. Remember to make a plain row between every two button rows.

If desired, the buttons may be made larger or smaller by making five or three chain stitches, but four will be found a good average number. They can also be easily arranged in rows or groups according to the taste of the worker. A common and effective arrangement popular just now on covers for baby carriages is in groups of diamonds. The covers are crocheted in Afghan stitch in strips of two different colors, as white and blue, each about four inches wide. On the white strips are worked diamonds of blue buttons, and on the blue strips diamonds of white buttons. In this case the buttons are worked every row close together and gradually increasing from one to the widest part of the diamond, and then diminishing again regularly to one. In passing the diamond two threads are carried along, one being used for the buttons, the other for the ground work of the stripe.

Instead of being made in working backwards with the Afghan stitch, the buttons or picots may also be formed while raising the stitches. Thus, after raising a vertical stitch in the ordinary way, make three or four chain stitches, take the hook out of the last loop, insert it once again in the vertical stitch, and pull the last chain through, and proceed to raise the next stitch.

Another form of button is made in ordinary treble crochet, and is much used for borders to various articles. To make these proceed as follows:

Make a chain of the length of the proposed border. Then in the first row work two treble stitches. In the next stitch work eight trebles; take the hook out of the last, put it in the first of the eight and insert it successively in each stitch—whipping them over, as it were. Then catch the wool, pull it through all the loops on the needle, and finish with a chain stitch. Make three treble stitches, then another button. Break off the wool at the end of every row. In the second row work four trebles, then a button, and so on, making a button every fourth stitch.

BABY'S BIB.

It is worked with white Knitting Cotton No. 10, with a fine hook in ribbed (DC.) crochet, the same stitch used for Table Mats only of course it is much finer.

Make a chain of 38 stitches, widening in the middle, by making 2 stitches in the 19th loop. Turn, and DC. back always throughout the work, put-

ting the hook in the outside half of the loop, and widening always in the middle.

Continue thus back and forth until you can count 13 of those "ribs," fasten and break off the cotton. Then make a new chain of 55 stitches and fasten it with the hook to the upper corner of the piece you have crocheted, (*opposite* the corner where you broke off the thread, to make the rib come right), crochet down the side of the bib, widen at the corner, then across the bottom, widening at the centre and at that corner, then crochet up the other side, and then make a chain of 55 stitches, without breaking off the thread.

Turn, work back around the bib, and out to the end of the chain on the other side, always widening at the corners and in the middle, and always taking the back part of the loop.

Continue this until you can count 8 ribs on the side; then finish with any pretty edge you may fancy, and put cord and tassel of the cotton on to tie it on with.

CROCHET EDGINGS.

FIRST PATTERN.

Make a chain of 15 stitches.

1st row: 1 treble into 6th chain, 4 chain, pass 4, 1 treble into each of 5 successive chain stitches; turn.

2d row: 6 chain, 1 treble into each of 5 trebles of last row, 2 chain, pass 2, 1 treble into the next 5 successive stitches, 2 chain, 1 treble into 3d chain of loop made in 1st row; turn.

3d row: 5 chain, 1 treble into 1st of 5 trebles in last row, 4 chain, 5 trebles under 2 chain of last row; turn.

Repeat from 2d row until you have the required length.

SECOND PATTERN.

Make a chain of 15 stitches.

1st row: 1 treble into the 6th chain, * 3 chain, pass 2 chain, 1 treble into 3d chain, repeat twice from *; turn.

2d row: 5 chain, * 3 trebles into 3 chain in preceding row, 1 chain; repeat twice from *; 0 trebles into loop made of 6 chain; turn.

3d row: 3 chain, 1 treble between 1st 2 trebles in preceding row, * 2 chain, 1 treble between the next 2 trebles, 1 treble between the next 2 trebles; repeat 3 times from *; 3 chain, 1 treble into the 1 chain between 3 trebles at once from the last *, then 3 chain, 1 treble between last 2 trebles; turn.

4th row: 3 chain, * 3 trebles into 3 chain of last row, 1 chain; repeat twice from *; 2 trebles, 2 chain, 2 trebles into space made by 2 chain between 2 trebles; repeat 3 times from the last *; turn.

5th row: 1 single crochet, 4 trebles, 1 single into each 2 chain of last row 4 times; 6 chain, 1 treble into 1 chain between 2 trebles and 1st 3 trebles of last row; * 3 chain, 1 treble between 3 trebles; repeat once from *; 3 chain, 1 treble between last 2 trebles: turn.

Repeat from 2d row until you have the required length.

A CHILD'S PETTICOAT.

Children's undergarments, both knitted and crocheted, are very popular now. The cut represents a pretty little petticoat in ribbed crochet which is easily and quickly made. It is worked in pink and white Saxony wool with a bone crochet hook.

Begin at the lower edge with a chain a yard and a quarter in length, and divisible by 12, the number for each scallop, which is dented thus:

Work from right to left. * 1 DC on each of the first 5 ch., 3 DC into the sixth, for the centre and outward peak; 5 DC on the next 5 ch., miss 2 to

12 treble in 1st of the 3 treble made in 3d row; join with 1 single crochet to the treble made in 1st row; 1 single crochet, 1 chain in each stitch all around the edge of shell, ending with single crochet. This completes the scallops.

Commence with 3 chain, 3 treble in hole, etc., until the required length.

In each scallop after the first, after the 12 treble, join to the last single crochet and the edge of preceding scallop.

RAISED LEAF TIDY.

Cast on 13 stitches.

First row: Knit 4 plain, 2 purl, over twice, one plain, over twice, 2 purl, 4 plain.

Second row: 6 plain, 5 purl, 6 plain.

shape the hollow or inner peak; this at the same time makes an open seam, which divides the scallops. Repeat from *, and, at the end of the row, to rib the crochet, turn the work, and pierce the needle at the back of the stitch in the preceding line.

At the 20th row decrease by missing 1 stitch on either side of the festoon. Fasten off at the 32d row, and join at the back, leaving a placket hole or not as preferred. Prepare a band of double crochet, on which work any simple crochet edging. A drawing string may be inserted through this.

SHELL-EDGING CROCHET.

Make a chain of 8 stitches. 1st row—Miss 3, 3 treble in chain, 2 chain, 1 treble in 1st stitch of chain. 2d row—Turn, 3 chain, 3 treble in hole made in 1st row, 2 chain, 1 treble in the 1st of the 3 treble made in 1st row. 3d row—Same as 2d. 4th row—Turn, 3 chain, 3 treble in last hole made; 3 chain,

Third row: 4 plain, 2 purl, 2 plain, over twice, 1 plain, over twice, 2 plain, 2 purl, 4 plain.

Fourth row: 6 plain, 9 purl, 6 plain.

Fifth row: 4 plain, 2 purl, 4 plain, over twice, 1 plain, over twice, 4 plain, 2 purl, 4 plain.

Sixth row: 6 plain, 13 purl, 6 plain.

Seventh row: 4 plain, 2 purl, 11 plain, narrow, 2 purl, 4 plain.

Eighth row: 6 plain, 12 purl, 6 plain.

Ninth row: 4 plain, 2 purl, 10 plain, narrow, 2 purl, 4 plain.

Tenth row: 6 plain, 11 purl, 6 plain.

Eleventh row: 4 plain, 2 purl, 9 plain, narrow, 2 purl, 4 plain.

Twelfth row: 6 plain, 10 purl, 6 plain.

Thirteenth row: 4 plain, 2 purl, 8 plain, narrow, 2 purl, 4 plain.

Fourteenth row: 6 plain, 9 purl, 6 plain.

Fifteenth row: 4 plain, 2 purl, 7 plain, narrow, 2 purl, 4 plain.

Sixteenth row: 6 plain, 8 purl, 6 plain.

Seventeenth row: 4 plain, 2 purl, 6 plain, narrow, 2 purl, 4 plain.

Eighteenth row : 6 plain, 7 purl, 6 plain.

Nineteenth row : 4 plain, 2 purl, 5 plain, narrow, 2 purl, 4 plain.

Twentieth row : 6 plain. 6 purl, 6 plain.

Twenty-first row : 4 plain, 2 purl, 4 plain, narrow, 2 purl, 4 plain.

Twenty-second row : 6 plain, 5 purl, 6 plain.

Twenty-third row : 4 plain, 2 purl, 3 plain, narrow, 2 purl, 4 plain.

Twenty-fourth row : 6 plain, 4 purl, 6 plain.

Twenty-fifth row : 4 plain, 2 purl, 2 plain, narrow, 2 purl, 4 plain.

Twenty-sixth row : 6 plain, 2 purl, 6 plain.

Twenty-seventh row : 4 plain, 2 purl, narrow, 2 purl, 4 plain.

Repeat from first row as many times as required for the length desired. Finish each strip separately by crocheting around them, and then crochet or sew them together. By adding two stitches more on each side ("thread over twice and purl two together"), and by casting on 2 stitches, at the beginning and widening one every time across until you have the thirteen stitches you can finish each point with a tassel. In the first six rows, if the first stitch of "over twice" is plain the second is purl, and vice versa.

<hr>

TORCHON LACE,

Cast on 13 stitches.

1st row : Slip 1, knit 2, over and knit 2 together 4 times, over, knit 2 plain.

2d row : Slip 1, knit rest plain.

3d row : Slip 1, knit 3, over and knit 2 together 4 times, over, knit 2 plain.

4th row : Same as second.

5th row : Slip 1, knit 4, over and knit 2 together 4 times, over, knit 2 plain.

6th row : Same as second.

7th row : Slip 1, knit 5, over and knit 2 together 4 times, over, knit 2 plain.

8th row : Same as second.

9th row : Slip 1, knit 6, over and knit 2 together 4 times, over, knit 2 plain.

10th row : Like second.

11th row : Slip 1, knit 7, over and knit 2 together times, over, knit 2 plain.

12th row : Like second.

13th row : Slip 1, knit 8, over and knit 2 together 4 times, over, knit 2 plain.

14th and 15th rows plain.

16th row : Slip 1, knit 2 together, over and knit 2 together 5 times, knit 6 plain.

17th row : Plain.

18th row : Slip 1, knit 2 together, over and knit 2 together 5 times, knit 5 plain.

19th row : Plain.

20th row : Slip 1, knit 2 together, over and knit 2 together 5 times, knit 4 plain.

21st row : Plain.

22d row : Slip 1, knit 2 together, over and knit 2 together 5 times, knit 3 plain.

23d row : Plain.

24th row : Slip 1, knit 2 together, over and knit 2 together 5 times, knit 2 plain.

25th row : Plain.

26th row : Slip 1, knit 2 together, over and knit 2 together 5 times, knit 1 plain.

27th and 28th rows : Plain.

This completes the pattern. Repeat from first row.

<hr>

INFANT'S KNITTED SHIRT.

One skein of cream white Shetland wool. Two quite fine bone needles. The following are the directions for one-half of the garment, which is joined under the arms :

1. Cast on 82 stitches.

2. Purl across.

3. Knit across plain.

4. Slip off first stitch, narrow 1, 2 plain, thread over and knit 1, thread over and knit 2, narrow 2, knit 2, thread over and knit 1, thread over and knit 2, narrow 2, knit 2, etc., across.

5. Purl across.

6. Same as 4.

7. Knit across plain.

8. Purl across.

9. Knit across plain.

10. Begin at 4 and so on to 10 until you have four times knitted the inclusive rows, and you will have four rows of scallops, which form the bottom of the shirt.

Then knit 2 plain, purl 2, 2 plain, purl 2, and so across. Make 45 rows in this manner, being careful to have them match, so as to give the work the appearance of seaming.

Cast on 16 stitches for the shoulder. Then knit across the entire width, shoulder and body. Purl across. Knit 2, thread over and knit 1, narrow 1, knit 2, etc., across. This last row makes a row of holes, through which narrow ribbon can be drawn to make the neck smaller, if desired. Bind off.

The sleeve is made of the four rows of scalloping in the same way as that round the bottom of the body, and joined to the shoulder.

<hr>

NORMANDY INSERTION.

Cast on 27 stitches.

First row : Slip 1, 4 plain, narrow, over, 3 plain, over, narrow, 4 plain, 1 twist st.

Second row : Slip 1, 3 plain, narrow, over, 5 plain, over, narrow, 2 plain, 1 twist st.

Third row : Slip 1, 2 plain, narrow, over, 1 plain, narrow, over, 1 plain, over, narrow, 1 plain, over, narrow, 2 plain, 1 twist st.

Fourth row : Slip 1, 1 plain, narrow, over, 1 plain,

narrow, over, 3 plain, over, narrow, 1 plain, over, narrow, 1 plain, 1 twist st.

Fifth row: Slip 1, narrow, over, 1 plain, narrow, over, 5 plain, over, narrow, 1 plain, over, narrow, 1 twist st.

Sixth row: Narrow, over, 1 plain, narrow, over, 3 plain, over, narrow, 2 plain, over, narrow, 1 plain, over, narrow.

Seventh row: Slip 1, over, narrow, 1 plain, over, narrow, 3 plain, narrow, over, 1 plain, narrow, over, 1 plain, 1 twist st.

Eighth row: Slip 1, 2 plain, over, narrow, 1 plain, over, narrow, 1 plain, narrow, over, 1 plain, narrow, over, 2 plain, 1 twist st.

Ninth row: Slip 1, 3 plain, over, narrow, 1 plain, over, slip 1, narrow and throw the slipped stitch over, over, 1 plain, narrow, over, 3 plain, 1 twist st.

Tenth row: Slip 1, 4 plain, over, narrow, 3 plain, narrow, over, 4 plain, 1 twist st.

Eleventh row: Slip 1, 5 plain, over, narrow, 1 plain, narrow, over, 5 plain, 1 twist st.

Twelfth row: Slip 1, 6 plain, over, knit 3 together, over, 6 plain, 1 twist st.

Repeat from the beginning.

A KNITTED BIB.

With No. 14 cotton and corresponding needles cast on 28 stitches, and knit one plain row. The third row knit 1 plain 1 purl throughout.

4th row: Purl the plain stitches and knit plain the purl ones, increasing one stitch at the end. This increase is made by knitting two loops into one.

5th row: Knit the purl stitches plain and purl the plain ones, increasing one stitch at the end.

Proceed in this manner for 20 rows, then knit 32 rows without any increase.

53d and 54th rows: Cast off at the beginning of each 6 stitches, increasing one at the end of the 54th.

55th to 69th rows: Like 4th and 5th, increasing one stitch at the end of each.

70th row: Increase both at the beg   and end of this row.

71st to 79th rows: Like 4th and 5th, increasing one stitch at the end of each row.

80th row: Increase both at beginning and end of row.

81st to 84th row: Same as 4th and 5th. There should now be 66 stitches on the needle.

85th row: Cast off 10 stitches in the middle, and work the two side pieces, of 28 stitches each, separately as follows:

1st row: Narrow three times on the neck side of the bib, and increase one stitch at the outer edge.

2d row: Plain and purl, without narrowings or increasings. Repeat these two rows 9 times more, making 20 rows in all. There are now 8 stitches left.

21st row: Knit two together throughout, and cast off on the next row.

Any simple edging may now be sewn around the sides and bottom of the bib. Remember that the narrow ribbing—knit 1, purl 1, etc.—is to be kept up throughout the work, and the increased stitches must be managed so as to fall in regularly with the pattern. Thus, supposing the last stitch is to be plain followed by an increase, then knit the first stitch in the loop plain and the increase purl. If the last is a purl stitch followed by an increase, then purl the first stitch and knit the increase plain. In this way the pattern will always run smoothly to the edges of the work.

The size of the bib will depend largely on that of the needles, and can be varied at pleasure.

A USEFUL PATTERN.

This pretty pattern is knitted in alternate stripes of open work, and is used for shawls, clouds, etc.

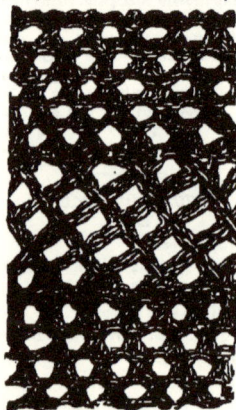

It is very easy. Cast on an uneven number of stitches, and knit them off plain.

1st row: Knit plain.

2d row: Purl knitting.

3d row: Slip the first stitch, * make 1, knit 2 together, repeat from * to the end of the row.

4th row: Knit plain.

5th row: Knit plain.

6th row: Purl.

7th row: Like 3d row.

Repeat from this row until you have five rows of holes. After the fifth repetition of the 3d row knit three rows plain.

23d row: Slip 1, make 1, * slip 1, knit 2, draw the slipped stitch over the two knitted ones, make 1, repeat from * to the end of the row.

24th row: Purl knitting; repeat these two rows 4 more times; in the last repetition knit the 2d row instead of purling it.

33d row: Slip 1, * make 1, knit 2 together, repeat from *.

34th row: Knit plain.

35th row: Knit plain.

36th row: Purl.

Repeat these four last rows four more times; then again begin at the 23d row. If this pattern is worked the length of a cloud it would look very well. Four hundred stitches should be cast on No. 0 needles for a cloud.

LACE MITTENS.

This mitten may be knitted long or short, and in any size. Use purse silk, white or black, and No. 14 needles. Cast on to 3 needles 60 stitches. Knit first 2 rounds plain.

3d round: Knit 2 together twice; * over twice, knit 1, over twice, knit 1, over twice, knit 1, over twice, knit 1, knit 2 together 4 times; repeat from *; at the close of the round knit 2 together twice.

4th round: Knit 2; on the double "over" stitch of the preceding row knit 1 only; knit the round plain, always knitting 1 on the double stitch.

Repeat these 2 rounds 6 more times for a short mitten; from 12 to 18 times for a long one.

You next commence the increasing for the thumb. You begin this between the first and last stitches of the round by making 1 stitch only; in the next round this is knitted. The rest of the pattern is carefully knitted as before.

In the 3d row of the thumb make 1 before and after this first stitch, so increasing the thumb to 3: knit them plain in the 4th row.

Increase each alternate round in this manner for the thumb until you have 24 extra stitches; then commence the thumb and end it by knitting 2 together twice, make 2, knit 4, knit 2 together 4 times, make 2, knit 4, knit 2 together twice; the 4 stitches knitted together must be in the centre of the thumb.

When you have the 24 stitches and the pattern properly arranged, knit 10 rounds on the thumb stitches only, using a third needle to join them; then 4 rounds plain and cast off.

You must now continue the hand part for 12 repetitions of the pattern; then knit 4 rounds plain, and cast off. The top of the mitten, the hand and the thumb are now edged with a little crochet border of this pattern:

1 treble on the 1st stitch, * 1 ch., miss 1, 1 treble in the next stitch, repeat from *.

2d row: 1 D.C. over the 1st ch., * 3 ch., 1 D.C. over the ch., repeat from *.

3d row: 1 D C. on the 2d of the first 3 Ch. * 3 ch., 1 D C. on the 2d of the next 3 ch.; repeat from * and fasten off at the end of the round.

NARROW EDGINGS.

WHEAT-EAR EDGE.—Cast on 5 stitches.

1st row: 2 plain, over, 1 plain, over twice, purl 2 together.

2d row: Over twice, purl 2 together, 4 plain.

3d row: 3 plain, over, knit 1, over twice, purl 2 together.

4th row: Over twice, purl 2 together, 5 plain.

5th row: 4 plain, over, knit 1, over twice, purl 2 together.

6th row: Over twice, purl 2 together, 6 plain.

7th row: 6 plain, over twice and purl 2 together.

8th row: Over twice and purl 2 together; 3 plain.

OX-HEART POINT.—Cast on 6 stitches.

1st row: Knit 1, over twice, purl 2 together, over 3 times, purl 2 together, over, knit 1.

2d row: Knit 2 together, knit 2, purl 1, knit 1, purl 1, knit 1.

The 3d and 4th, 5th and 6th, 7th and 8th rows are just like the 1st and 2d, except that with each couplet there is an increase of one more plain stitch at the head of the lace.

9th row: 9 plain, make 1, knit 1.

10th row: Knit 2 together, cast off 4, kit 5.

PINAFORE STITCH.

That popular and charming opera, H. M. S. Pinafore, has not only given many hours of delightful enjoyment to the music-loving public, but has left behind evidences of its popularity in the name of many small articles and ornaments. Even the world of crochet has not escaped its influence, for the Pinafore stitch is now well known and recognized among its workers. Although not exactly a new stitch, having a strong resemblance to an older member of the family known as chain and link, it is a useful stitch and one likely to be popular. It is a variety of the Afghan stitch, or crochet tricotée, and is worked as follows:

For experimental purposes make a chain of say fourteen stitches.

Raise each of the chains in the usual crochet tricotée manner, and work back thus: Catch the wool and draw it through the first stitch. * Make one chain. Catch the wool again and draw it through two. Make one chain, and draw it through four. Repeat from *. Make a chain and draw through two.

The raising of the stitches the next row is somewhat peculiar, and requires a little care when working from written instructions. The loop on the hook counts as the first stitch. On the left is the chain stitch binding together three of the upright stitches and forming a kind of eyelet. * Put the loop under the near right-hand half of this chain and raise a stitch. Next put it through the eyelet, under the further left-hand part of the chain, and raise another. Then put the hook under the near right-hand part of the next chain stitch—that made after drawing the wool through two loops—and raise a stitch; next raise the vertical stitch that follows it. Now comes the eyelet again. This is raised as before, repeating the directions from *. Raise the edge stitch in the usual way and work back as before.

The stitch when properly worked looks very much like star stitch, with the addition of a row of vertical stitches between every two stars. It is adopted to any kind of work for which the ordinary Afghan stitch can be used. The pattern, it will be seen, runs in groups of four, and a little study will show that it can easily be widened or narrowed.

NORMANDY LACE.

Cast on 31 stitches.

1st row : Knit 8, narrow, over 1, knit 3, over 1, narrow, knit 9, narrow, over 1, knit 3, over 1, purl last stitch and slip it back, over 1, knit 1.

2d row : Knit 2, over 1, knit 5, over 1, narrow, knit 7, narrow, over 1, knit 5, narrow, over 1, knit 7.

3d row : Knit 6, narrow, over 1, knit 7, over 1, narrow, knit 5, narrow, over 1, knit 1, narrow, over 1, knit 1, over 1, narrow, knit 1, over 1, purl last stitch, slip it back, over 1, knit 1.

4th row : Knit 2, over 1, knit 1, narrow, over 1, knit 3, over 1, narrow, knit 1, over 1, narrow, knit 3, narrow, over 1, knit 9, over 1, narrow, knit 5.

5th row: Knit 4, narrow, over 1, knit 11, over 1, narrow, knit 1, narrow, over 1, knit 1, narrow, over

1, knit 5, over 1, narrow, knit 1, over 1, purl last stitch, slip back, knit 1.

6th row : Knit 2, over 1, knit 1, narrow, over 1, knit 3, over 1, narrow; knit 2, over 1, narrow, knit 1, over 1, knit 3 together, over 1, knit 13, over 1, narrow, knit 3.

7th row : Knit 5, over 1, narrow, knit 9, narrow, over 1, knit 3, over 1, narrow, knit 1, over 1, narrow, knit 3, narrow, over 1, knit 1, narrow, over 1, knit 1, narrow.

8th row : Bind off 1, knit 1, over 1, narrow, knit 1, over 1, narrow, knit 1, narrow, over 1, knit 1, narrow, over 1, knit 5, over 1, narrow, knit 7, narrow, over 1, knit 6.

9th row : Knit 7, over 1, narrow, knit 5, narrow, over 1, knit 7, over 1, narrow, knit 1, over 1, slip 1, narrow. Slip the slipped stitch over the narrowed stitch, over 1, knit 1, narrow, over 1, knit 1, narrow.

10th row : Bind off 1, knit 1, over 1, narrow, knit 3, narrow, over 1, knit 9, over 1, narrow, knit 3, narrow, over 1, knit 8.

11th row : Knit 9, over 1, narrow, knit 1, narrow, over 1, knit 11, over 1, narrow, knit 1, narrow, over 1, knit 1, narrow.

12th row : Bind off 1, knit 1, over 1, knit 3 together, over 1, knit 13, over 1, knit 3 together, over 1, knit 10.

A SUMMER CLOUD.

A charming Summer cloud may be crocheted of Shetland floss wool worked in shell pattern, already described in The Tribune, and in the first number of The Woman's Extra in the directions for a small three-cornered shawl. A recent specimen intended for seaside wear was of a light blue, nearly three yards long and about two feet wide, and was edged all round with a plain row of scallops, each containing nine trebles. A chain of 361 stitches was first made. This allowed for sixty shells. Each shell was formed of six trebles, the wool being so fine that five trebles failed to make the shell full enough.

The second row was begun by a D. C. exactly in the middle of the first shell of the first row. It was ended by fastening the last shell of the second row in the middle of the last shell of the first row, and finishing with 3 chain.

The third row was begun by making 3 chain precisely in the same hole in which the second row started, and working in this same spot a shell of six trebles, finishing it with a D.C. on the middle of the first shell of the second row. At the end of this row, after making a D. C. on the top of the last shell of the second row, another shell was worked in the opening at the base of the 3 chain and was finished with a D. C. on the top of this 3 chain.

The second and third rows were repeated throughout. These modifications from the directions already given are necessary to prevent the cloud from widening or narrowing. In the instructions for a three-cornered shawl the work is all the time increasing in width. In the cloud the width is unchanged.

The cloud was worked with a hook about No. 8, and took twelve ounces of the floss. A fair worker sticking steadily at it should do it readily in two days. Using only odds and ends of time it would take a week or a fortnight.

A CROCHET SPREAD.

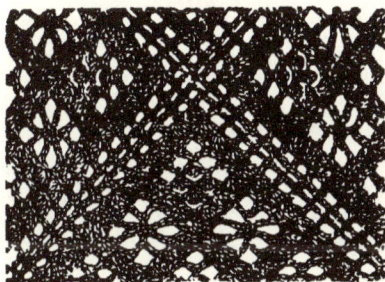

The spread, of which the cut above represents a part, consists of groups of large squares, each made up of twelve smaller ones. The diagram shows one-half of one of these larger squares, with the way in which they are joined. The spread may be worked in fine cotton or in single zephyr wool, with a No. 12 or 14 crochet hook.

Begin with a chain of 4 stitches, which join into a ring.

1st round. * 5 ch., 1 DC on the next chain, repeat from * twice, then 3 ch., 1 treble on the 4th ch.

2d round. 5 ch., 1 DC on the 3rd of the next 5 ch., * 5 ch., 1 DC on the 4th of the same 5 ch., 5 ch., 1 DC on the 3rd of the next 5 ch., repeat from * all round, ending with the extra loop in the corner.

3rd round. * 5 ch., 1 DC on the 3rd of the next 5 ch., 5 ch., 1 DC on the 3rd of the next 5 ch., 5 ch., 1 DC on the 4th of the same 5 ch., repeat from * three more times.

4th round. * 5 ch., 1 DC on the 3rd of the next 5 ch., 3 treble on the DC between the 2 loops of 5 ch., 1 DC on the 3rd of the next 5 ch., 5 ch., 1 DC on the 3rd of the next 5 ch., 5 ch., 1 DC on the 4th of the same 5 ch., repeat from * three more times.

5th round. * 5 ch., 1 DC on the 3rd of the next 5 ch., 3 treble on the next DC, 3 treble on the next DC, 1 DC on the 3rd of the next 5 ch., 5 ch., 1 DC on the 3rd of the next 5 ch., 5 ch., 1 DC on the 4th of the same 5 ch., repeat from * three more times.

6th round. * 5 ch., 1 DC on the 3rd of the next 5 ch., 3 treble on the next DC, 1 DC on the 2d of the next 3 treble, 5 ch., 1 DC on the 2nd of the next 3 treble, 3 treble on the next DC, 5 ch., 1 DO on the 3rd of the next 5 ch., 5 ch., 1 DC on the 4th of the same 5 ch., repeat from * 3 times.

7th round. * 5 ch., 1 DC on the 3rd of the next 5 ch., 3 treble on the next DC, 5 ch., 1 DC on the 3rd of the next 5 ch., 4 ch., 1 DC on the same stitch, 5 ch., 1 DC on the 2nd of the next 3 trebles, 1 DC on the 3rd of the next 5 ch., 5 ch., 1 DC on the 3rd of the next 5 ch., 5 ch., 1 DC on the 4th of the same 5 ch., repeat from * three more times.

8th round. * 5 ch., 1 DC on the 3rd of the next 5 ch., 3 treble on the next DC, 1 DC on the 2nd of the next 3 treble, 5 ch., 1 DC on the 3rd of the next 5 ch., 4 ch., 1 DC on the same stitch, 5 ch., 1 DC on the 3rd of the next 5 ch., 4 ch., 1 DC on the same stitch, 1 DC on the 2nd of the next 3 treble, 3 treble on the next DC, 5 ch., 1 DC on the 3rd of the next 5 ch., 5 ch., 1 DC on the 4th of the same 5 ch., repeat from * three more times.

9th round. * 5 ch., 1 DC on the 3rd of the next 5 ch., 3 treble on the next DC, 1 DC on the 3rd of the next 5 ch., 3 treble on the next DC, 1 DC on the 3rd of the next 5 ch., 5 ch., 1 DC on the 3rd of the next loop of 5 ch., 4ch., 1 DC on the same stitch, 5 ch., 1 DC on the 3rd of the next 5 ch., 3 treble on the next DC, 1 DC on the next 3 treble, 3 treble on the next DC, 5 ch., 1 DC on the 3rd of the next 5 ch., 1 DC on the 4th of the same 5 ch., repeat from * three more times.

10th round. * 5 ch., 1 DC on the 3rd of the next 5 ch., 3 treble on the next DC, 1 DC on the 2nd of the next 3 treble, 5 ch., 1 DC on the 2nd of the next 3 treble, 3 treble on the next DC, 1 DC on the 3rd of the next 5 ch., 5 ch., 1 DC on the 3rd of the next loop of 5 ch., 3 treble, 1 DC on the 2nd of the next 3 treble, 5 ch., 1 DC on the 2nd of the next 3 treble, 5 ch., 1 DC on the 3rd of the next 5 ch., 5 ch., 1 DC on the 4th of the same 5 ch., repeat from * three more times.

11th round. 5 ch., 1 DC on the 3rd of the next 5 ch., 3 treble on the next DC, 1 DC on the 2nd of the next 3 treble, 5 ch., 1 DC on the 3rd of the next 5 ch., 5 ch., 1 DC on the 3rd of the next 5 ch., 3 treble on the next DC, 1 DC on the 3rd of the next 5 ch., 3 treble on the next DC, 1 DC on the 2nd of the next 3 treble, 5 ch., 1 DC on the 3rd of the next 5 ch., 5 ch., 1 DC on the 2nd of the next 3 treble, 3 treble on the next DC, 5 ch., 1 DC on the 3rd of the next 5 ch., 5 ch., 1 DC on the 4th of the next 5 ch., repeat from * three more times.

12th round. 5 ch., 1 DC on the 3rd of the next 5 ch., 3 treble on the next DC, 1 DC on the 2nd of the next 3 treble, 5 ch., 1 DC on the 3rd of the next 5 ch., 1 ch., 1 DC on the next DC, 1 ch., 1 DC on 3rd of the next 5 ch., 5 ch., 1 DC on the 2nd of the next 3 trebles, 3 trebles on the next DC, 1 DC on the 2nd of the next 3 trebles, 5 ch., 1 DC on the 3rd of the next 5 ch., 1 ch., 1 DC on the next DC, 1 ch., 1 DC on the 3rd of the next 5 ch., 5 ch., 1 DC on the 2nd of the next 3 treble, 3 trebles on the next DC, 1 DC on the 3rd of the next 5 ch., 5ch., 1 DC on the 3rd of the next 5 ch., 5 ch., 1 DC on the 4th of the same 5 ch., repeat from * three more times.

13th round. 5 ch., 1 DC on the 3rd of the next 5 ch., 3 treble on the next DC, 1 DC on the 2nd of the next 3 treble, 3 treble on the next DC, 1 DC on the 3rd of the next 5 ch., 5 ch., 1 DC on the 2nd of the next 3 DC, 5 ch., 1 DC on the 3rd of the next 5 ch., 3 treble on the next DC, 1 DC on the 2nd of the next 3 treble, 3 treble on the next DC, 1 DC on the 3rd of the next 5 ch., 5 ch., 1 DC on the 2nd of the next 3 DC, 5 ch., 1 DC on the 3rd of the next 5 ch., 3 treble on the next DC, 1 DC on the 2nd of the next 3 treble, 3 treble on the next DC, 1 DC on the 3rd of the next 5 ch., 5 ch., 1 DC on the 3rd of the next 5 ch., 5 ch., 1 DC on the 4th of the same 5 ch., repeat from * three times.

14th round. 5 ch., 1 DC on the 3rd of the next 5 ch., 3 treble on the next 1 DC, DC on the 2nd of the next 3 treble, 5 ch., 1 DC on the 2nd of the next 3 treble, 3 treble on the next DC, 1 DC on the 3rd of the next 5 ch., 5 ch., 1 DC on the 3rd of the following 5 ch., 3 treble on the next DC, 1 DC on the 2nd of the next 3 treble, 5 ch., 1 DC on the 2nd of the next 3 treble, 3 treble on the next DC, 1 DC on the 3rd of the next 5 ch., 5 ch., 1 DC on the 3rd of the next 5 ch., 3 treble on the next DC, 1 DC on the 2nd of the next 3 treble, 5 ch., 1 DC on the 2nd of the next 3 treble, 3 treble on the next DC, 1 DC on the next 5 ch., 5 ch., 1 DC on the 3rd of the next 5 ch., 5 ch., 1 DC on the 4th of the same 5 ch., repeat from * three more times.

15th round. 5 ch., 1 DC in the 3rd of the next 5 ch., 3 treble on the next DC, 1 DC on the 2nd of the next 3 treble, 5 ch., 1 DC on the 3rd of the next 5 ch., 4 ch., 1 DC on the same stitch, 5 ch., 1DC on the 2nd of the next 3 treble, 3 treble on the next DC, 1 DC on the 3rd of the next 5 ch., 3 treble on the next DC., 1 DC on the 2nd of the next 3 treble, 5 ch., 1 DC on the 3rd of the next 5 ch., 4 ch., 1 DC on the same stitch, 5 ch., 1 DC on the 2nd of the next 3 treble, 3 treble on the next DC, 1 DC on the 2nd of the next 5 ch., 3 treble on the next DC, 1 DC on the 2nd of the next 3 treble, 5 ch., 1 DC on the 3rd of the next 5 ch., 5 ch., 1 DC on the 2nd of the next 3 treble, 3 treble on the next DC, 5 ch., 1 DC on the 3rd of the next 5 ch., 5 ch., 1 DC on the 4th of the same 5 ch., repeat from * three more times.

16th round. In this round you join the squares by passing the 2nd of each 5 ch., and the 2nd of each 3 treble, through the corresponding stitches in other squares, * 5 ch., 1 DC on the 3rd of the next 5 ch., 3 treble on the next DC, 1 DC on the 2nd of the next 3 treble, then 5 ch., 1 DC on the 3rd of the next 5 ch., three times, 3 treble on the next DC, 1 DC on the 2nd of the next 3 treble, then 5 ch., 1 DC on the 3rd of the next 5 ch., three times, 3 treble on the next DC, 1 DC on the 2nd of the next 3 treble, then 5 ch., 1 DC on the 3rd of the next 5 ch., three times, 3 treble on the next DC, 1 DC on the 2nd of the next 3 treble, then 5 ch., 1 DC on the 3rd of the next 5 ch., three times, 3 treble on the next DC, 1 DC on the 3rd of the same 5 ch., repeat three times from *, and fasten off securely.

MOSS MATS.

With single zephyr in five shades of scarlet, beginning with the lightest shade. make a round mat in treble crochet increasing enough to make it round and flat, until it is of the size you wish. Then with three shades of green, beginning with the darkest, cast on medium size steel knitting needles 11 stitches and knit plain a strip in each shade long enough to go around the outside of the mat. When the three strips are completed dip them into boiling water and dry quickly. Then sew the darkest strip on the edge of the mat, the next shade so that it will meet the lower edge of the outer row of crocheting, and the lightest strip upon the edge of the next row of crocheting.

Then ravel out the knitted strips, leaving one stitch in each row at the edge sewed to the centre. This forms a curly moss all round the mat. White daisies or cherries in wool are pretty placed in this moss.

OLIVE LEAF PATTERN.

Counterpanes, tidies and the like are knit in stripes as well as in squares, and a combination of both forms is often exceedingly effective. The following stripe may, for example, be used between the rows of large squares of the Raised Leaf Pattern :

Cast on 38 stitches with 4 extra for edge stitches —2 on each side.

1st row : Knit 2, purl 2, * narrow (by knitting 2 together), knit 11, purl 2, over twice, knit 1, over twice, purl 2, repeat from * ; knit 2.

2d row : Knit 2, knit 2, * purl 3, knit 2, purl 10, purl 2 together, knit 2, repeat from * ; knit 2.

Remember that the second loop of the " over twice " is to be dropped throughout the pattern. Also that in " over twice " before a purl stitch the cotton is brought forward and then carried twice around the needle.

3d row : Knit 2, purl 2, *narrow, knit 9, purl 2, knit 1, over, knit 1, over, knit 1, purl 2, repeat from * ; knit 2.

4th row : Knit 2, knit 2, * purl 5, knit 2, purl 8, purl 2 together, knit 2, repeat from * ; knit 2.

5th row : Knit 2, purl 2, * narrow, knit 7, purl 2, knit 2, over, knit 1, over, knit 2, purl 2, repeat from * ; knit 2.

6th row : Knit 2, knit 2, * purl 7, knit 2, purl 6, purl 2 together, knit 2, repeat from * ; knit 2.

7th row : Knit 2, purl 2, *narrow, knit 5, purl 2, knit 3, over, knit 1, over, knit 3, purl 2, repeat from *, knit 2.

8th row : Knit 2, knit 2, *purl 9, knit 2, purl 4, purl 2 together, knit 2, repeat from *, knit 2.

9th row : Knit 2, purl 2, *narrow, knit 3, purl 2, knit 4, over, knit 1, over, knit 4, purl 2, repeat from*; knit 2.

10th row : Knit 2, knit 2, *purl 11, knit 2, purl 2, purl 2 together, knit 2, repeat from*; knit 2.

11th row : Knit 2, purl 2 * narrow, knit 1, purl 2, knit 5, over, knit 1, over, knit 5, purl 2. repeat from * knit 2.

12th row : Knit 2, knit 2, * purl 13, knit 2, purl 2 together, knit 2, repeat from *, knit 2.

13th row : Knit 2, purl 2, *over twice, knit 1,

over twice, purl 2, narrow. knit 11, purl 2, repeat from °, knit 2.

14th row : Knit 2, knit 2, °purl 10, purl 2 together, knit 2, purl 3, knit 2, repeat from °; knit 2.

15th row : Knit 2, purl 2, °knit 1, over, knit 1, over, knit 1, purl 2, narrow, knit 9, purl 2, repeat from°, knit 2.

16th row : Knit 2, knit 2, °purl 8, purl 2 together, knit 2, purl 5, knit 2, repeat from°, knit 2.

17th row : Knit 2, purl 2, °, knit 2, over, knit 1, over, knit 2, narrow, knit 7, purl 2, repeat from °; knit 2.

18th row : Knit 2, knit 2, °. purl 6, purl 2 together, knit 2, purl 7, knit 2, repeat from °; knit 2.

19th row : Knit 2, purl 2 °, knit 3, over, knit 1, over, knit 3, purl 2, narrow, knit 5, purl 2, repeat from °; knit 2.

20th row : Knit 2, knit 2, ° purl 4, purl 2 together, knit 2, purl 9, knit 2, repeat from °; knit 2.

21st row : Knit 2, purl 2, ° knit 4, over, knit 1, over, knit 4, purl 2, narrow, knit 3, purl 2, repeat from °; knit 2.

22d row : Knit 2, knit 2, ° purl 2, purl 2 together, knit 2, purl 11, knit 2, repeat from °; knit 2.

23d row : Knit 2, purl 2, °knit 5, over, knit 1, over, knit 5, purl 2, narrow, knit 1, purl 2, repeat from °; knit 2.

24th row : Knit 2, knit 2, ° purl 2 together, knit 2, purl 13, knit 2, repeat from ° ; knit 2.

Repeat from the beginning. If a wider stripe is desired add 18 stitches for each additional pattern, and repeat the directions between the stars for every pattern added.

KNITTED FRINGE.

A handsome and easily-worked fringe for the decoration of furniture, and allied uses, may be acceptable to many readers. It is made of double zephyr wool. The band at the top may be knitted with black, and the fringe portion of various colors arranged to suit individual tastes, or the special article to which the fringe is applied. A good plan is to run regularly through half a dozen different shades of the same color before changing. The wool for the fringe portion should be cut into lengths of nine or ten inches, or according to the depth desired.

With the black or other selected color, and No. 10 or 11 needles, cast on nine stitches and knit across plain.

On the second row knit 2 plain, then insert one of the lengths of the fringe between the two needles, one-half of it being in front of the work, and the other half behind it. Now knit 2 more plain stitches, and bring the lower half of the fringe between the needles to the front. Knit 2 more plain stitches and put both ends of the fringe from the front to the back, passing them of course between the needles. Knit two more plain stitches and bring both ends of the fringe to the front again. Knit the last stitch plain.

Knit back plain.

The fourth row is knit exactly like the second, the second and third rows being repeated till the fringe is long enough.

LACE PATTERN.

Cast on 30 stitches.

1st row : Slip 1, knit 1, over, narrow (or knit 2 together), slip the second stitch on the left needle over the first and continue to do so until you have slipped 4 ; over 4, knit 4, over 1, narrow, s. b. 4 ("slip back 4"), over 4, knit 4, over, narrow, knit 1, over 2, narrow, over 2, narrow, knit 1.

2d row Slip 1, knit 2, purl 1, knit 2, purl 1, knit 2, over, narrow, knit 4, purl 1, knit 1, purl 1, knit 1, over, narrow, knit 4, purl 1, knit 1, purl 1, knit 1, over, narrow, knit 1.

3d row : Slip 1, knit 1, over, narrow, knit 8, over, narrow, knit 8, over, narrow, knit 8.

4th row : Slip 1, knit 8, over, narrow, s. b. 4,

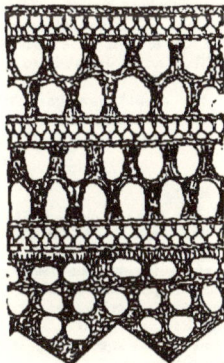

over 8. knit 4, over, narrow, s. b. 4, over 4, knit 4, over, narrow, knit 1.

5th row: Slip 1, knit 1, over, narrow, knit 4, purl 1, knit 1, purl 1, knit 1, over, narrow, knit 4, purl 1, knit 1, purl 1, knit 1, over, narrow, knit 1, over 2, narrow, over 2, narrow, over 2, narrow, knit 1.

6th row: Slip 1, knit 2, purl 1, knit 2, purl 1, knit 2, purl 1, knit 2, over, narrow, knit 8, over, narrow, knit 8, over, narrow, knit 1.

7th row : Slip 1, knit 1, over, narrow, s. b. 4, over 4, knit 4, over, narrow, s. b. 4, over 4, knit 4, over, narrow, knit 1.

8th row : Slip 1, knit 11, over, narrow, knit 4, purl 1, knit 1, purl 1, knit 1, over, narrow, knit 4, purl 1, knit 1, purl 1, knit 1, over, narrow, knit 1.

9th row : Slip 1, knit 1, over, narrow, knit 8, over, narrow, knit 8, over, narrow, knit 4, over 2, narrow, over 2, narrow, knit 3.

10th row : Slip 1, knit 4, purl 1, knit 2, purl 1,

knit 5, over. narrow, a, b. 4, over 4, knit 4, over, narrow, a. b. 4, over 4, knit 4, over, narrow, knit 1.

11th row: Slip 1, knit 1, over, narrow, knit 4, purl 1, knit 1, over, narrow, knit 4, purl 1, knit 1, purl 1, knit 1, over, narrow, knit 13.

12th row: Cast off 7, knit 6, over, narrow, knit 8, over, narrow, knit 8, over, narrow. knit 1.

KNITTED LACE.

This edging is excellent for all washing articles, as it is strong and does not stretch. Cast on 8 stitches and knit across plain.

1st row: Slip 1 with the thread before the needle as in purling: put the thread back and knit 1, over, knit 2 together, knit 2 plain, over twice, knit the rest plain.

2d row: Slip 1 as above, then knit plain till you come to the long loop made by "over twice;" knit the 1st, purl the 2d, the rest knit plain.

3d row: Slip 1, knit 1, over, knit 2 together, knit the rest plain.

4th row: Slip 1, the rest plain.

5th row: Slip 1, knit 1, thread forward, knit 2 together, knit 2, over twice, the rest plain. Knit the 6th row like the 2nd, and the 7th row like the 4th.

8th row: You should now have 12 stitches. Cast off four, being careful to slip the 1st, as in purling. This makes the pattern. Begin again at 1st row.

No. 2.

Cast on 16 stitches.

1st row: Knit 3, make 1, purl 2 together, knit 1, make 2, narrow, knit 4, make 2, narrow, make 1, purl 2 together.

2d row: Make 1 (by putting needle under the thread and throwing the thread around the needle), purl 2 together, knit 2, purl 1, knit 6, purl 1, knit 1, make 1, purl 2 together, knit 3.

3d row: Knit 3, make 1, purl 2 together, knit 11, make 1, purl 2 together.

4th row: Make 1, purl 2 together, knit 11, make 1, purl 2 together, knit 3.

5th row: Knit 3, make 1, purl 2 together, knit 1, make 2 and narrow twice, knit 4, make 2, narrow, make 1, purl 2 together.

6th row: Make 1, purl 2 together, knit 2, purl 1, knit 6, purl 1, knit 2, purl 1, knit 1, make 1, purl 2 together, knit 3.

7th row: Knit 3, make 1, purl 2 together, knit 14, make 1, purl 2 together.

8th row: Make 1, purl 2 together, knit 14, make 1, purl 2 together, knit 3.

9th row: Knit 3, make 1, purl 2 together, knit 1, make 2, narrow, make 2, knit 3 together, make 2 and narrow 4 times, make 1, purl 2 together.

10th row: Make 1, purl 2 together, knit 2 and purl 16 times, knit 1, make 1, purl 2 together, knit 3.

11th row: Knit 3, make 1, purl 2 together, knit 10, make 1, purl 2 together.

12th row: Bind off 10 stitches, leaving 15 on left

---

needle, knit 10, make 1, purl 2 together, knit 3. Repeat 1st row

---

TIDY IN KNITTING.

Take cotton No. 12, 14 or 16. Every alternate row is to be purled except 3 stitches on each edge, which are always to be knitted plain.

Cast on 11 stitches for each pattern and 6 more for the edge. Ninety-four stitches will make a tidy of medium width.

Knit 3 plain rows to begin.

1st pattern row: Knit 3 (edge) stitches, *, knit 3 together, knit 1, over, knit 3, over, knit 2 together twice; repeat from *.

2d row: Purl; 3 stitches plain on each edge. Every alternate row the same as the second.

3d row: Knit 2 together, over, knit 2 together, knit 1, over, knit 1, over, knit 2 together, knit 1, over, knit 2 together, repeat.

5th row: Knit 2 together, knit 2, over, knit 3, over, knit 2, knit 2 together, repeat.

7th row: Knit 2 together, knit 1, over, knit 5, over, knit 1, knit 2 together; repeat.

9th row: Knit 2 together, over, knit 1, over, knit 2 together, knit 1, knit 2 together, over, knit 1, over, knit 2 together; repeat.

11th row: Knit 1, over, knit 2 together, knit 1, over, knit 3 together, over, knit 2 together, knit 1, over, knit 1; repeat.

13th row: Knit 1,* over, knit 3, knit 2 together, knit 4, over, knit 2 together: repeat from.*

15th row: Knit 1, over, knit 1, over, knit 2 together 4 times, over, knit 1, over; repeat.

17th row: Knit 1, over, knit 2 together, knit 1, over, knit 2 together twice, over, knit 2 together, knit 1, over; repeat.

19th row: Knit 2, over, knit 2. knit 2 together twice, knit 2, over, knit 1; repeat.

21st row: Knit 3, over, knit 1, knit 2 together twice, knit 1, over, knit 2; repeat.

23d row: Knit 1, knit 2 together, over, knit 1, over, knit 2 together twice, over, knit 1, over, knit 2 together; repeat.

25th row: Knit 2 together, over, knit 2 together, knit 1, over, knit 2 together, over, knit 2 together, knit 1, over; repeat.

27th row: Knit 1, knit 2 together, knit 2, over, knit 1, over, knit 2, knit 2 together, knit 1; repeat

Begin again at 1st pattern row, and repeat the pattern to the length you wish.

FLUTED LACE.

Cast on 18 stitches.

1st row: *Knit across plain.

2d row: Purl 14; this leaves 4 stitches on the left needle; turn the work as if to begin at the end of the needle.

3d row: Slip the first of the 14 stitches from the left needle on to the right one; knit 9, narrow, over, knit 2.

4th row: Purl 14; turn the work as in 2d row.

5th row : Slip the 1st of the 14 stitches as in 3d row ; knit 13 ; this ends the 1st quill or fluting.

Now begin the 2d :

1st row : Knit plain across.

2d row : Knit 4, purl 14.

3d row : Knit 1, narrow, over, knit 11 ; turn the work.

4th row : Slip the 1st of the 14 stitches as before, knit 13.

5th row : Knit 18 across plain*. Repeat from first * to the last, thus making 2 quills. This lace can be made of any width desired for children's ruffles. The addition must be made in the plain work, the edges remaining as above.

CROCHET PATTERN.

This crocheted strip is nice for clouds, blankets, rugs, etc., if worked in thick wools—the thick part of the stripe is not effective in thin wools.

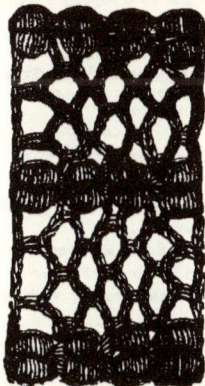

Make a chain of 20 stitches for the foundation.

1st row : 3 ch., then a tufted long stitch. This is made by putting the wool 10 or 11 times round the needle, then put the needle into the 4th ch. from the needle, draw the needle through all the stitches on it at once ; put the wool 11 times round the needle again, take up the next stitch and finish in the same manner. Then 2 ch., miss 2, 1 DC on the next stitch of the foundation, 5 ch., miss 3, 1 DC on the next 3 ch., then a twisted long stitch on the 3d and 4th ch. from the last DC, 3 ch., miss 2 ch., a DC on the next, 5 ch., miss 3 ch., a DC on the next, 3 ch., a twisted long stich on the 2d and 1st ch. of the foundation, 3 ch., turn.

2d row : A twisted long stitch on each of the 2 twisted stitches underneath, 2 ch., 1 DC on the 2d of the three chain, 5 ch., 1 DC on the 3d of the five chain, 5 ch., 1 twisted long on each of the twisted stitches in the last row, 5 ch., 1 DC on the middle of the next loop of 5 ch , 5 ch., a twisted long on each of the two twisted stitches at the end of the row.

3d row : Turn, 3 ch., a twisted long on each of the two first stitches, 3 ch., 1 DC on the 3d of the next 5 ch., 5 ch., a DC in the middle stitch of the next loop, 3 ch., a twisted stitch on each of the two next twisted stitches, 3 ch., a DC on the 3d of the next 5 ch., 5 ch., a DC in the middle of the next loop, 3 ch., a twisted long on each of the two twisted long stitches at the end of the row. Repeat the last two rows the length the pattern is required.

BABY'S COUVRETTE.

This pattern makes a series of holes, and is pretty knitted in white with narrow blue or pink ribbon run through the holes, and with bows at the corners.

Cast on any number of stitches which can be divided by seven.

1st row : Thread forward, slip 1, knit 1, pass the slipped stitch over the knitted one, knit 5

2d row : Purl.

3d row : Thread forward, slip 1, knit 1, pass slipped stitch over, knit 1, purl 3, knit 1.

4th row : Purl 1, knit 1, thread forward, knit 2 together, purl 3.

5th row : Thread forward, slip 1, knit 1, pass slipped stitch over, knit 1, purl 3, knit 1.

6th row : Purl.

7th row : Thread forward, slip 1, knit 1, pass slipped stitch over, knit 5.

8th row : Purl.

Begin again at 3d row.

CHATELEINE BAG.

This pretty bag covered with jet beads is knitted plain. The beads must first be threaded on moderately coarse black purse twist.

Cast on 5 stitches. 1st row : Plain knitting. Begin every row by putting the silk round the needle to increase.

2d row : Increase ; knit the first stitch, insert the needle in the next and push up 1 bead or two if you like. Push up 2 with every stitch except the last.

3d row : Plain knitting. Always increase at the beginning and don't let the beads slip to the wrong side.

4th row : Push up the beads as before with every stitch except the first and last.

When you have increased your knitting to the width of 4½ inches or as broad as you desire your bag to be, stop the increasings. Now count your stitches for reference afterward. Continue the plain and beaded rows alternately until the work is 5 inches long, not counting the pointed part. Decrease by knitting 2 at the beginning of every row to match the commencement.

For the other side or back of the bag, begin with the same number of stitches you had when directed to count ; do a square of 5 inches ; decrease for the point.

If you prefer the back without beads stop

pushing them up after you have knitted the first point which forms the flap of the bag. To make up the bag sew the sides together, and line with black silk; line the flap neatly also; add a fastening with elastic and a jet button.

If you wish the bag to have more shape, make the back silk lining double and insert card-board or stiff muslin between.

Thread a needle with the silk and add a fringe all the way round by threading about 16 beads and stitching them to the sides of the bags in loops. Do the same to the flap.

Sew ribbon to each side and end off with a bow, under which a large hook must be sewn, to fasten the bag to the belt.

POINT-LACE PATTERN.

Cast on 15 stitches.

First row : Knit 3, over, slip 1, knit 2 together, pull the slipped stitch over, over, knit 3, over, knit 2 together, over twice, knit 2 together, over twice, knit 2 together.

Second row : Over, knit 2, purl 1, knit 2, purl 1, knit 1, purl 6, knit 1, over, knit 2 together knit 1.

Third row : Knit 3, over, knit 2 together, over, knit 2 together, knit 1, knit 2 together, over, knit 8.

Fourth row : Cast off 3, knit 4, purl 6, knit 1, over knit 2 together, knit 1.

Fifth row : Knit 3, over, knit 2 together, knit 1, over, slip 1, knit 2 together, pull the slipped stitch over, over, knit 2, over twice, knit 2 together, over twice, knit 2 together.

Sixth row : Over, knit 2, purl 1, knit 2, purl 1, knit 1, purl 6, knit 1, over, knit 2 together, knit 1.

Seventh row : Knit 3, over, knit 2 together, knit 2 together, over, knit 1, over, knit 2 together, knit 8.

Eighth row : Cast off 3, knit 4, purl 6, knit 1, over, knit 2 together, knit 1.

Begin again at the first row.

VALENCIENNES LACE.

Cast on 16 stitches.

First row : Knit 3, over twice, purl 2 together, knit 2, over twice, knit 2 together, over twice, knit 2 together, knit 5.

Second row : Knit 7, purl 1, knit 2, purl 1, knit 2, over twice, purl 2 together, knit 3.

Third row : Knit 3, over twice, purl 2 together, knit 13.

Fourth row : Knit 13, over twice, purl 2 together, knit 3.

Fifth row : Knit 3, over twice, purl 2 together, knit 2, over twice, knit 2 together, over twice, knit 2 together, over twice, knit 2 together, knit 5.

Sixth row : Knit 7, purl 1, knit 2, purl 1, knit 2, purl 1, knit 2, over twice, purl 2 together, knit 3.

Seventh row : Knit 3, over twice, purl 2 together, knit 16.

Eighth row : Cast off 5, knit 10, over twice, purl 2 together, knit 3. -

Begin again at the first row. In this pattern, "over twice" before a purl stitch means to bring the cotton forward and turn it over around the needle.

A PRETTY EDGING.

Cast on 14 stitches.

First row : Slip 1, knit 1, over, narrow, 1 plain, over and knit 2 together 4 times, 1 plain.

2d row : First make 1, then knit across plain. Every alternate row the same.

3d row : Slip 1, knit 1, over, narrow, 2 plain, over and knit 2 together 4 times, 1 plain.

5th row : The same as 3d, only 3 plain, over and knit 2 together 4 times, 1 plain.

7th row : The same as 3d, only 4 plain, over and knit 2 together 4 times, 1 plain.

9th row : The same as 3d, only 5 plain, over and knit 2 together 4 times, 1 plain.

11th row : The same as 3d, only 6 plain.

12th row : Cast off 5, knit the remaining stitches plain. Begin at 1st row.

HONEYCOMB PATTERN.

Cast on any number of stitches divisible by 7 : add an odd stitch.

Always slip the first stitch of every row, besides the two slipped stitches, which are not knit at all until the 8th row, when the whole row is knit across.

1st row : Pick off the 1st stitch*, slip 2, knit 1, thread over, narrow, knit 1*; repeat from* to * to the end of the row, which must end as it commenced, with slip 2, knit 1.

2d row : Like the 1st, except that it is knit purl-wise with the thread in front, and instead of thread over it is thrown around the needle.

3d row : Like the 1st.

4th row : Like the 2d.

5th row : Like the 1st; this brings the wrong side of the work next to you.

6th row : Knit plain across; knitting the slipped stiches which have not before.

7th row : Purl.

8th row : Plain. This makes half the pattern.

The 9th row is similar to the first, except that you commence with slip 1*, thread over, narrow, knit 1, slip 2, knit 1*; continue from * to *.

10th row : The same, knit purlwise.

11th row : The same as 9th

12th row : Like 10th.

13th row : Same as the 9th.

14th row : Plain across.

15th row : Purl across.

16th row : Plain. This completes the pattern. You commence again at the 1st row.

RAISED LEAF PATTERN.

The odds and ends of time during the long Summer days can often be used by economic workers in knitting squares, or shells, or stripes which can afterward be sewn together into useful and handsome counterpanes, tidies, toilet covers, pin cushions, mats etc. The coarseness or fineness of the cotton and needles may be left to the taste of the knitter, but as a general rule No. 8 cotton and No. 14 needles may be used for the coarser work, and No. 18 cotton and No. 16 needles for the finer. In every case care should bo taken to proportion the cotton to the size of the needles.

A pretty pattern in squares is known as the Raised Leaf pattern, and is worked thus:

Cast on one stitch.

1st row: Over, knit 1.
2d row: Over, knit 2.
3d row: Over, knit 1, over, knit 1, over, knit 1.
4th row: Over, knit 1, purl 3, knit 2.
5th row: Over, knit 3, over, knit 1, over, knit 3.
6th row: Over, knit 2, purl 5, knit 3.
7th row: Over, knit 5, over, knit 1, over, knit 5.
8th row: Over, knit 3, purl 7, knit 4.
9th row: Over, knit 7, over, knit 1, over, knit 7.
10th row: Over, knit 4, purl 9, knit 5.
11th row: Over, knit 9, over, knit 1, over, knit 9.
12th row: Over, knit 5, purl 11, knit 6.
13th row: Over, knit 11, over, knit 1, over, knit 11.
14th row: Over, knit 6, purl 13, knit 7.
15th row: Over, knit 13, over, knit 1, over, knit 13.
16th row: Over, knit 7, purl 15, knit 8.
17th row: Over, knit 15, over, knit 1, over, knit 15.
18th row: Over, knit 8, purl 17, knit 9.
19th row: Over, knit 9, narrow (by knitting 2 together), knit 13, slip 1, knit 1 and throw the slipped stitch over, knit 9.
20th row: Over, knit 0, purl 15, knit 10.
21st row: Over, knit 10, narrow, knit 11, slip 1, knit 1 and throw slipped stitch over, knit 10.
22d row: Over, knit 10, purl 13, knit 11.
23d row: Over, knit 11, narow, knit 9, slip 1, knit 1 and throw slipped stitch over, knit 11.
24th row: Over, knit 11, purl 11, knit 12.
25th row: Over, knit 12, narrow, knit 7, slip 1, knit 1 and throw slipped stitch over, knit 12.
26th row: Over, knit 12, purl 9, knit 13.
27th row: Over, knit 13, narrow, knit 5, slip 1, knit 1 and throw slipped stitch over, knit 13.
28th row: Over, knit 13, purl 7, knit 14.
29th row: Over, knit 14, narrow, knit 3, slip 1, knit 1 and throw slipped stitch over, knit 14.
30th row: Over, knit 14, purl 5, knit 15.
31st row: Over, knit 15, narrow, knit 1, slip 1, knit 1 and throw slipped stitch over, knit 15.
32d row: Over, knit 15, purl 3, knit 16.
33d row: Over, knit 17, narrow, knit 16.
34th row: Over, knit 16, purl 2, knit 17.
35th row: Over, knit 17, narrow, knit 17.

36th row: Purl throughout.
37th and 38th rows: Narrow, rest plain.
39th row: Narrow, rest purl.

Continue as from 37th, two plain rows and one purl—always remembering to narrow at the beginning of each row—till there is only one stitch left. Cast off. This completes one square.

In arranging the pattern four leaves should be brought to one point, and the squares should be sewn together as flatly as possible without dragging. The joining of the larger squares thus formed requires no special direction.

COUNTERPANE—STAR PATTERN.

This is one of the square patterns. Cast on 50 stitches. For the border knit 10 rows plain, and in order to save repetition knit 8 stitches plain at the beginning and ending of every row of the pattern proper, which will thus consist of 34 stitches.

1st row: Purl 9, knit 1, purl 14, knit 1, purl 9.
2d and every even row up to the 20th: Plain.
3d row: Purl 9, knit 2, purl 12, knit 2, purl 9.
5th row: Purl 9, knit 3, purl 10, knit 3, purl 9.
7th row: Purl 9, knit 4, purl 8, knit 4, purl 9.
9th row: Purl 9, knit 5, purl 6, knit 5, purl 9.
11th row: Purl 9, knit 6, purl 4, knit 6, purl 9.
13th row: Purl 9, knit 7, purl 2, knit 7, purl 9.
15th row: Purl 9, knit 16, purl 9.
17th row: Purl 1, knit 15, purl 2, knit 15, purl 1.
19th row: Purl 2, knit 13, purl 4, knit 13, purl 2.
21st row: Purl 3, knit 11, purl 6, knit 11, purl 3.
22d, 24th, 26th and 28th rows: Knit 15, purl 4, knit 15.
23d row: Purl 4, knit 9, purl 2, knit 4, purl 2, knit 9, purl 4.
25th row: Purl 5, knit 7, purl 3, knit 4, purl 3, knit 7, purl 5.
27th row: Purl 6, knit 5, purl 4, knit 4, purl 4, knit 5, purl 6.
29th row: Purl 7, knit 3, purl 1, knit 4, purl 4, knit 4, purl 1, knit 3, purl 7.
30th, 32d and 34th rows: Knit 11, purl 4, knit 4, purl 4, knit 11.
31st row: Purl 8, knit 1, purl 2, knit 4, purl 4, knit 4, purl 2, knit 1, purl 8.
33d row: Purl 8, knit 1, purl 2, knit 4, purl 4, knit 4, purl 2, knit 1, purl 8.
35th row: Purl 7, knit 3, purl 1, knit 4, purl 4, knit 4, purl 1, knit 3, purl 7.
36th row: Knit 10, purl 1, knit 4, purl 4, knit 4, purl 1, knit 10.
37th row: Purl 6, knit 5, purl 4, knit 4, purl 4, knit 5, purl 6.
38th, 40th and 42d rows: Knit 15, purl 4, knit 15.
39th row: Purl 5, knit 7, purl 3, knit 4, purl 3, knit 7, purl 5.
41st row: Purl 4, knit 9, purl 2, knit 4, purl 2, knit 9, purl 4.
43d row: Purl 3, knit 11, purl 6, knit 11, purl 3.
44th, and every even row to the 62d, plain.
45th row: Purl 2, knit 13, purl 4, knit 13, purl 2.

47th row: Purl 1, knit 15, purl 2, knit 15, purl 1.
40th row: Purl 9, knit 16, purl 9.
51st row: Purl 9, knit 7, purl 2, knit 7, purl 9.
53d row: Purl 9, knit 6, purl 4, knit 6, purl 9.
55th row: Purl 9, knit 5, purl 6, knit 5, purl 9.
57th row: Purl 9, knit 4, purl 8, knit 4, purl 9.
59th row: Purl 9, knit 3, purl 10, knit 3, purl 9.
61st row: Purl 9, knit 2, purl 12, knit 2, purl 9.
63d row: Purl 9, knit 1, purl 14, knit 1, purl 9.
Finish off with 10 plain rows to complete the border. This makes one square. It will be noticed that this is not an open pattern, but that the star is made by the contrast of plain and purl stitches. Patterns worked in this way are often exceedingly pretty.

KNITTING PATTERN.

This is particularly pretty, applied to clouds and

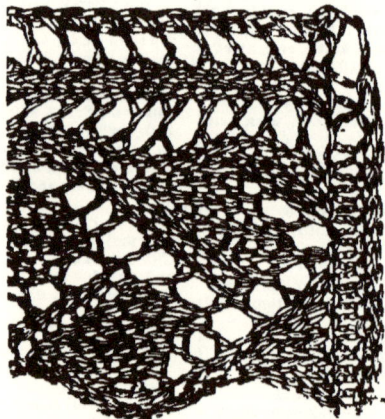

shawls. Eighteen stitches are required for each pattern.

Knit four rows plain.

1st pattern row: Slip 1, * make 1, knit 2 together knit 1, make 1, knit 2 together, knit 2, make 1 knit 1, make 1, knit 2 together, knit 3, knit 2 together, knit 1; repeat from *.

2d row: Purl knitting. 3d row: Slip 1, * make 1, knit 2 together, knit 1, make 1, knit 2 together, knit 2, make 1, knit 3, make 1, knit 1, knit 2 together, knit 1, knit 2 together, knit 1; repeat from *.

4th row: Purl knitting. 5th row: Slip 1, * make 1, knit 2 together, knit 1, make 1, knit 2 together, knit 2, make 1, knit 5, make 1, knit 1, knit 3 together, knit 1; repeat from *.

6th row: Purl knitting. 7th row: Slip 1, * make 1, knit 2 together, knit 1, make 1, knit 2 together, knit 3, knit 2 together, knit 1, make 1, knit 1, make 1, knit 3; repeat from *.

8th row: Purl knitting. 9th row: Slip 1, * make

1, knit 2 together, knit 1, make 1, knit 2 together, knit 2 together, knit 1, knit 2 together, knit 1, make 1, knit 3, make 1, knit 3, repeat from *.

10th row: Purl knitting. 11th row: Slip 1, * make 1, knit 2 together, knit 1, make 1, knit 2 together, knit 3, knit 1, make 1, knit 3, make 1, knit 3; repeat from *.

12th row: Purl knitting. With the 13th row begin again as with 1st row.

LACE IN TWO WIDTHS.

Wide Lace.—Cast on 35 stitches. Knit across plain twice.

1st row: Slip 1, knit 10, over, knit 2 together, knit 3, over, knit 2 together, knit 3, over, knit 2 together, over, knit 2 together, over, knit 1.

2d row: Knit plain.

3d row: Slip 1, knit 20, over, knit 2 together, knit 3, over, knit 2 together, knit 3, over, knit 2 together, over, knit 2 together, over, knit 1.

4th row: Knit plain.

5th row: Slip 1, knit 21, over, knit 2 together, knit 3, over, knit 2 together, knit 3, over, knit 2 together, over, knit 2 together, over, knit 1.

6th row: Knit plain.

7th row: Slip 1, knit the rest plain.

8th row: Knit 2 together twice; then cast the first stitch on the right hand needle over the second, leaving one stitch upon that needle; knit the rest plain. Repeat from 1st row.

Narrow Lace.—Cast on 20 stitches and knit across plain twice.

1st row: Slip 1, knit 9, over, knit 2 together, knit 3, over, knit 2 together, over, knit 2 together, over, knit 1.

2d row: Knit plain.

3d row: Slip 1, knit 10, over, knit 2 together,

knit 3, over, knit 2 together, over, knit 2 together, over, knit 1.

4th row : Knit plain.

5th row : Slip 1, knit 11, over, knit 2 together, knit 3, over, knit 2 together, over, knit 2 together, over, knit 1.

6th row : Knit plain.

7th row : Slip 1, knit the rest plain.

8th row : Knit 2 together, knit 2 together, slip the first stitch on the right hand needle over the second, leaving one stitch upon that needle ; knit the rest plain.

Repeat from 1st row. Use fine thread and needles.

FLY FRINGE.

For tidies, shawls, mats and other articles, whether knitted or crocheted, a simple and common edging, known in the shops as "fly fringe," may be made as follows :

When several yards of it are required take two studs or nails on opposite sides of a room or as far apart as may be desired. With the cotton or wool to be used, fasten to one of the studs and wind the material around the two studs half a dozen times, or more if a heavy fly is wanted.

Now take the ball and tie tightly round the loose strands, as they may be called, of this long rope, just below the first stud or nail. Make another tie three-quarters of an inch or an inch lower, not cutting off the thread, but making a tight double hitch. Repeat these double hitches at the same intervals till the second stud is reached.

Next take a pair of scissors and between each tie cut the threads through, all except the one which was used to make the ties. This remains intact from the beginning to the end. The other threads, when severed, form little tufts, bound together by the ties at regular intervals, very much like the insertions in the tail of a boy's kite. The tufts, or flies, can be made larger or smaller by increasing or diminishing the number of threads wound around the studs, and can be placed any distance apart by regulating the double hitches or ties. The fringe can obviously be made of any particular color, or mixture of colors.

JULIA PATTERN.

This is a pretty pattern for counterpanes or covers for baby carriages, done either in stripes or squares with double zephyr. In cotton it is not so effective.

Make a chain of any uneven number of stitches.

1st and 2d rows : Ordinary Afghan or crochet tricotee stitch.

3d row : Raise the first, * raise the next, then raise the one underneath on the first row. Pull the wool through the lower one, then through the next two loops ; then make 1 chain. Raise the next stitch as usual. Repeat from *.

4th and 5th rows : Crochet tricotee.

6th row : Like 3d.

Repeat these three rows throughout. The appearance of the stitch can be varied in alternate stripes or squares by changing the position of the "lumps" or raised stitches—those which stand out above the general level of the work. These can be arranged in rows or groups, or, in fact, after any desired pattern.

PALM LEAF LACE.

Cast on 10 stitches and knit across plain.

1st row : Slip 1, knit 1, over, narrow, over, narrow, over 3 times, narrow, over twice, purl 2 together.

2d row : Over twice, purl 2 together, knit 2, purl 1, in the next loop knit 1 and purl 1 (that is, after drawing the thread through in knitting and before slipping off the stitch bring the thread forward, and purl a stitch in the same loop : knit 1, purl 1, knit 1, purl 1, knit 2.

3d row : Slip 1, knit 1, over, narrow, knit 1, over, narrow, knit 4, over twice, purl 2 together.

4th row : Over twice, purl 2 together, knit 0, purl 1, knit 2, purl 1, knit 2.

5th row : Slip 1, knit 1, over, narrow, knit 2, over, narrow, knit 3, over twice, purl 2 together.

6th row : Over twice, purl 2 together, knit 4, purl 1, knit 3, purl 1, knit 2.

7th row : Slip 1, knit 1, over, narrow, knit 3, over, narrow, knit 2, over twice, purl 2 together.

8th row : Over twice, purl 2 together, knit 3, purl 1, knit 4, purl 1, knit 2.

9th row : Slip 1, knit 1, over, narrow, knit 4, over, narrow, knit 1, over twice, purl 2 together.

10th row : Over twice, purl 2 together, knit 2, purl 1, knit 5, purl 1, knit 2.

11th row : Slip 1, knit 1, over, narrow, knit 5, over, narrow, over twice, purl 2 together.

12th row : Bind off 3, then take the stitch on the right hand needle and put back on to the left hand needle ; then over twice, purl 2 together, knit 5, purl 1, knit 2.

CORAL AND LEAF EDGING.

Cast on 10 stitches.

1st row : 2 plain, over, 1 plain, over, 1 plain, slip 1, knit 2 together and throw slip stitch over ; 1 plain, over, 1 plain, over, narrow, 1 plain, over twice, 1 plain, over twice, narrow, 1 plain.

2d row : Slip 1, 2 plain, purl 2, 1 plain, purl to end of row.

3d row : 2 plain, over, 3 plain, slip 1, knit 2 together and throw slip stitch over, then over, 1 plain, over, 1 plain, over, narrow twice, 1 plain, over twice, narrow, over twice, narrow, 1 plain.

4th row : Same as 2d.

5th row : 3 plain, slip 1, knit 2 together, and throw slipped stitch over, over, 1 plain, over, narrow, 1 plain, narrow, 1 plain, over twice, narrow, over twice, narrow, 1 plain.

6th row : Same as second row.

7th row : 2 plain, over, slip 1, knit 2 together and

throw slipped over, 3 plain, over, 3 plain, over. 1 plain, over, narrow, plain to end of row.

8th row: Slip 1, cast off 9. This leaves 1 stitch on right needle and 15 stitches on left, all of which are to be purled.

Repeat from 1st row. To see the beauty of the pattern it requires several scallops to be knit.

SCRAP-BAG.

BICYCLE CAP.—A pretty bicycle cap for man or boy can he made by crocheting around the crown exactly like the well-known pattern for a star mat. Make a straight band to go round the head in double crochet, and sew to the crown. Wool, silk or cotton may be used for this cap.

COLORED STRIPE FOR AFGHAN OR BED-SPREAD.— Cast on 30 stitches on wooden needles. Knit plain to middle stitch and narrow once each side of it, widening at beginning and end of each needle, one stitch.

Knit 30 times across, and put on the other color. Then, after 30 times with that color, put on the original, and so on till long as desired. After a sufficient number of stripes are knit crochet them together. This is simple enough for a child, and very pretty.

TRIMMING FOR FLANNEL.—Mrs. A. P. wishes to know what material to use for flannel skirts. Many persons use Shetland wool, but she will find that fine Saxony yarn is as pretty and wears better. To "slip" a stitch is to merely take a stitch off the left needle on to the right needle without knitting it. "Over," is made by putting the thread around the right needle so that an extra stitch is made.

TWIST-STITCH.—Miss M., Stockbridge, Mich., asks what is meant by "twist-stitch" in knitting. It is a stitch made by knitting from the back part of the loop. The right needle is put in behind the left needle, and passes through the loop from right to left much the same as in purling, except that in purling the needle is passed though the front part of the loop.

HONEYCOMB STITCH.—Cast on any number. 1st row, purl 1, slip 1, make 1, repeat; 2d row, slip 1, make 1, purl 2 together, repeat. At the end of the row purl 1 after purling 2 together.

3d: Purl 2, slip 1, repeat.

4th: Purl 2 together, slip 1, make 1, repeat. At the end of the row purl 1, instead of purling 2 together.

5th: Purl 1*, slip 1, purl 2, repeat from *.
Repeat from 2d row.

HERRING-BONE STITCH.—Cast on any number that will divide by 6. Knit 3 rows: 2d row purl, 1st and 3d plain. 4th row: Knit plain with the thread 8 times over the needle. 5th row: Slip off the first 6 stitches the full length, pass the 4th,

5th, and 6th through the first 3, then knit plain the 4th, 5th and 6th, then the 1st, 2d and 3d. Take off every 6 stitches in this way and knit the whole row. Repeat.

EDGINGS.—A. C. B. writes: In knitting edgings you will find that if the first stitch is slipped, the edge will be very much better than if it is knitted. In knitting the Normandy lace I found the pattern (by my knitting) not quite distinct enough in the growing part of the point; so I twisted the next to the last stitch, which made it perfect. There is a great deal of difference in different persons' hand-knitting—I don't know why we may not say *hand-knitting* as well as hand-writing."

ROMAN "SCARF" AFGHAN.—Set up 51 stitches. 1st row: Take the back of the first stitch and make 2; knit 25 stitches; then knit 2 together; then knit on to the end of the row. Always widen on the end at which you begin, and narrow in the middle: this will bring the colors to a point in the middle. If the pattern is used for a tidy you must have fine needles; if for an Afghan, large needles. When putting the stripes together the colors must be matched, and the effect will be very artistic. In knitting in the colors proceed thus: Knit 2 rows black; then 2 yellow; 2 black; 20 red; 28 gray or brown; 1 row yellow; 1 black; 5 rows red; 1 black; 3 blue; 1 red; 1 black; 3 yellow; 1 red; 1 white; 3 black; 1 red; 1 black; 6 green; 1 black; 1 white; 20 red; 28 gray or brown. Use Germantown wool.

THAT PUZZLING STAR.—Mrs Mary Harnick is much perplexed over the use of the star in knitting patterns. She has no trouble with other patterns, but when the * comes in she gets all wrong, etc., etc. The use of the * is really simple. It saves space in the directions, and prevents the repetition of many needless words. An illustration will perhaps make the point clearer to Mrs. H. Suppose she is knitting a row of 24 stitches in that simple open pattern formed by making an over and knitting two stitches together with two stitches on each side for edge stitches. She would first knit 2 (for the edge), then make an over, then knit 2 together, then an over, then knit 2 together, then another over followed by knit 2 together, and so on, making an over and knitting two together alternately till the last two stitches (for the edge) were reached. These should be knitted plain. Now using the star the directions for all this would be: Knit 2, * over, knit 2 together, repeat form * 9 times; knit 2. When Mrs. H. has mastered this she will have no further trouble about the stars. But she must remember that the * does not mean that the "*work* is to be turned." That would make a frightful mess of it.

CLOVER-LEAF EDGING.—Mrs. L. C. J. says: "I don't understand how any one can fail to make Mrs. Gideon's clover-leaf edging, her directions are so plain. It was my first attempt to crochet from printed directions, and I succeeded the first time of trying. I have made an alteration which'l think an improvement, viz.: DC instead of 'long treble,' on the foundation chain. A fine hook and No. 40 thread crocheted that way makes what any-o-o who sees it says is a 'beautiful trimming.'"

Mrs C.'s suggestion in regard to a kindred art has been for long under the consideration of this department and will be discussed as soon as possible.

PRETTY CROCHETED EDGING.—Minnie E. T. kindly writes: "I have knit and crocheted several of the edgings given in your excellent paper, and found some very handsome patterns. I have an edging quite different from any I have seen. It is simple and quite pretty. For the first vandyke make a chain of 6 stitches, miss 4, and in 5th chain make 1 D C. This forms a loop; turn. 3 chain and 3 trebles in this first loop; turn. 3 chain and 3 treble in the 2d loop formed by the 3 chain before worked; turn, 3 chain and 12 treble in the 3d loop and join the last one of the 12 treble to the first loop of 6 chain; turn, and work 2 chain and 1 D C. be-tween 9 of the 12 trebles, leaving 3 trebles.

2d vandyke: 3 chain and 3 trebles in the next loop; turn, 3 chain and 3 trebles in the next loop; turn, 3 chain and 12 trebles in the next loop, and join last treble to last 2 chain worked in the 1st van-dyke; turn, 2 chain and 1 D C. between 9 of the 12 trebles, leaving 3 trebles.

Work on as 2d vandyke until your edging is of sufficient length.

CROCHET SHAWLS.—For a round shawl begin in the centre on a chain of 5, and work a round of loops of 4 ch.; 1 DC. in the centre. Increase at in-tervals to keep the work in shape. Use needles No. 10, and fine wool. The 3d round is worked in loops of 5 ch., 1 DC. in the middle of the loop underneath.—4th round. " 3 treble worked as one on the first loop, 5 ch.; repeat from " on each loop. This row is worked throughout; it is increased by making two loops in one a second stitch " is 3 treble, 1 ch., 3 treble in the first loop, a DC. in the 2d; repeat from ". In the rows following the treble stitches are worked over the chain divid-ing the set below. For a square shawl, a very pretty shawl may be worked in alternate rows of color, and forms a checked appearance by the following: A chain the length required, 1st row: " 1 treble on the 3d and 4th stitches, 1 treble on the 1st and 2d stitches, 4 ch., miss 4 stitches; repeat from " on the next 4, fasten off at the end of the row. The following row is worked by 1 treble on the 1st stitch in the row, 3 ch., " 1 treble on the 3d and 4th of the next ch., 1 treble on the 1st and 2d of the 4 ch., then 4 ch.; repeat from ".

FLANNEL EDGING.—Cast on 6 stitches. 1st row: Slip 1, knit 1, over, knit 2 together, over, 2 plain.

2d row: Knit plain. Repeat these rows until you have 12 stitches; in repeating the 1st row knit plain to the last four stitches, then yarn over, 2 to-gether, etc.

12th row: Slip 1, knit 2 together, over, knit 2 to-gether, over, knit 2 together, knit the rest plain.

13th row: Knit plain. Repeat these last 2 rows until you have put six stitches on the needle, then commence at 1st row. This sample is knit with Angola yarn on fine stocking needles.

ALENCON LACE.—This is a very pretty narrow lace, light and open in pattern. Cast on 10 stitches.

1st row: Knit 3, over, narrow, over twice, nar-row, over twice, narrow, knit 1.

2d row: Begin by throwing the thread over the right needle to make a stitch, then knit 3, purl 1, knit 2, purl 1, knit 2, over, narrow, knit 1.

3d row: Knit 3, over, narrow, knit 8.

4th row: Bind off 3 stitches, knit 6, over, nar-row, knit 1.

Repeat from 1st row.

FLANNEL TRIMMING.—Cast on 10 stitches. 1st row: Knit plain. 2d row: Purl. 3d row: Slip 1, knit 1, " over, knit 2 together; repeat twice from ", over, knit plain to end of row. Re-peat this 3d row till you have 20 stitches on the needle, then slip 1, knit 2 together, " over, knit 2 together, repeat from " 3 times and knit plain to the end of the row. Repeat till there are only 10 stitches on needle. This makes one scollop. Make the lace as long as you please. U. T. C. wants a pattern for crocheted hood for infant; also one for a knitted shirt. Probably that in THE WEEKLY TRIBUNE of May 12 would suit her.

OPEN-WORK WRIST FOR GLOVE.—Cast on 26 stitches.

1st row: Knit plain.

2d row: Slip 1, over twice, knit 2 together, over twice, knit 2 together; continue thus to end of row.

3d row: Slip 1, knit 2, drop 1, knit 2, drop 1, knit 2; continue to end of row.

4th row: Knit plain. 5th row: Purl. 6th row: Knit plain. 7th row: Knit plain; this is the begin-ning of second pattern.

KNITTED EDGING.—Cast on 10 stitches.

1st row: Knit 2, over, narrow, over twice, nar-row, knit 4 plain.

2d row: Knit 6, purl 1, knit 1, purl 1, knit 2.

3d row: Knit 2, over, narrow, knit 7.

4th row: Knit 8, purl 1, knit 2.

5th row: Knit 2, over, narrow, over twice, nar-row, over twice, knit 3, narrow. With the left needle draw over the last stitch 3 stitches from the right needle (or cast off),

6th row: Knit 2, purl 1, knit 2, purl 1, knit 1, purl 1, knit 2.

7th row: Knit 2, over, narrow, knit the rest of the row plain.

8th row: Knit plain to the loop or "over" stitch, purl that, then knit 2 plain.

Begin again at 1st row.

CROCHET EDGING.—This edging may be worked with cotton, Nos. 22, 26 or 30, according to the purpose for which it is required, but looks best done with the finer number. It is commenced by making * 4 Ch. and 8C. into the 1st; repeat from * for the length desired. Then for the 1st row. 8C. on the first stitch of the first 4 Ch. of the foundation, * 5 Ch., passing over the two next little scollops, 1 treble (thread twice over the needle) on the following 8C., 4 Ch., 1 treble, into the same stitch as before, 5 Ch., passing over two scollops, 8C. on the next 8C. of foundation; repeat from *.—2d row. 1 DC on the 4th of the 5 Ch. of last row, 3 Ch., 2 8C. on the 2d and 3d of the following 4 Ch., 3 Ch., 1 DC on the 2d of next 5 Ch., 5 Ch.; repeat from *.—3d row. 1 DC on the 1st DC of last row* * 4 Ch., 1 8C. between the next 2 8C.. 4 Ch., 1 DC on the DC of last row, and a double on the following one; repeat from *.—4th row. 1 DC on the 1st DC of last row, * 4 Ch., 5 8C. on the 8C. of last row and the 2 Ch. on each side of it, 4 Ch., 1 DC taken into space between 2 doubles of last row; repeat from *.—5th row. * 8C. on the 2d of the 4 Ch. of last row, 4 Ch., 3 8C. on the 3 centre stitches of the 5 8C. of 4th row, 4 Ch., 8C. on the 3d of the next 4 Ch., 3 Ch.; repeat from *.—6th row. 8C. on the 1st 8C. of former row, * Ch., draw the thread through the 2d of the next 3 8C. and the loop on the needle, and proceed to work 5 trebles into the 1 8C. on the 3d row; then draw the thread through the same 2d stitch of the 3 8C. of last row and the loop on the needle, which will close up the group of trebles 5 Ch., 8C. into centre stitch of 3 Ch. of last row; repeat from *.—7th row. 8C. on the 3d of 1st 5 Ch. of last row, 5 Ch., 8C., taken between the two loops drawn through the centre stitch of 3 8C. of 5th row, 5 Ch., 8C. on the 3d of next 5 Ch., 5 Ch.; repeat from *.

CROCHETED AFGHAN. — Make a chain one and a quarter yards long, crochet 6 DC, miss 2, then 6 DC and 3 DC in the 7th stitch. This forms one scollop and is to be repeated across the chain. Turn and crochet DC in each back stitch. Always miss the 2 stitches in the same place and crochet the 3 in the centre of the highest points each time across. It is lovely made in light shades of Germantown, and it would be handsome in the same colors used for the "Roman Afghan." This department is pleased that N. A. P. enjoyed the novel sent to her. It will always be glad to print her patterns. Many responses have been received to her request for the early chapters of "Probation." If she will mention the dates and numbers of the papers she wants, one of these kind readers will send them to her. L. A. C. says: "There is something in the few words she has written that has gone straight to my heart, and I would like to say to her, 'Be hopeful; bear your sickness one day at a time, and may God in His loving kindness give you, as he has me, after being long an invalid, a moderate degree of health and a heart made tender and mindful of the sufferings of others.'"

SIMPLE POINT LACE.—For a pretty open-work point lace, nearly similar to the first example published in THE TRIBUNE, "Needlemaker" kindly sends the following directions:

Cast on 12 stitches.

First row: Knit 3 plain, over and knit 2 together 4 times, knit 1 plain.

Second row: Put thread over needle, knit rest plain.

Third row: Knit 4 plain, over and knit 2 together 4 times, knit 1 plain.

Fourth row: Same as 2d.

Fifth row: Knit 5 plain, over and knit 2 together 4 times, knit 1 plain.

Sixth row: Same as 2d.

Seventh row: Knit 6 plain, over and knit 2 together 4 times, knit 1 plain.

Eighth row: Same as 2d.

Ninth row: Knit 7 plain, over and knit 2 together 4 times, knit 1 plain.

Tenth row: Same as 2d.

Eleventh row: Knit 8 plain, over and knit 2 together 4 times, knit 1 plain.

Twelfth row: Same as 2d.

Thirteenth row: Plain.

Fourteenth row: Cast off all but 11 stitches, knit these plain. This completes the pattern.

MRS. J. C. W.'s SPREAD.—G. E. L. writes that she is making this spread and that after she had made a good many pieces she found easily how it is put together. M. H. W. says that she has succeeded in knitting a piece which answers nicely for an edge or border for this quilt. This department is indebted to her for her inclosed sample and for the following directions for making this border:

Cast on 33 stitches.

1st row: Knit plain.

2d row: Purl.

3d row: Knit 1, knit 2 together, knit 11, knit 2 together, over, knit 1, over, knit 2 together, knit 11, knit 2 together, knit 1.

4th row and every alternate row, purl.

5th row: Knit 1, knit 2 together, knit 9, knit 2 together, over, knit 1, over, knit 2 together 2 times, knit 9, knit 2 together, knit 1.

7th row: Knit 1, knit 2 together, knit 7, knit 2 together, over, knit 1, over, knit 2 together 3 times, knit 7, knit 2 together, knit 1.

9th row: Knit 1, knit 2 together, knit 5, knit 2 together, over, knit 1, over, knit 2 together 4 times, knit 5, knit 2 together, knit 1.

11th row: Knit 1, knit 2 together, knit 3, knit 2 together, over, knit 1, over, knit 2 together 5 times, knit 3, knit 2 together, knit 1.

13th row: Knit 1, knit 2 together, knit 1, knit 2 together, over, knit 1, over, knit 2 together 6 times, knit 1, knit 2 together, knit 1.

15th row: Knit 1, knit 2 together, knit 1, over, knit 1, over, knit 2 together 7 times, knit 2.

17th row: Knit 1, knit 2 together, over, knit 1, over, knit 2 together 7 times, knit 2 together, knit 1.

18th row: Purl the first 2 and last 2 together, then cast off.

THE NEW-YORK TRIBUNE.

AN AMAZING PREMIUM.

On the terms named below, THE TRIBUNE will send to agents and subscribers, *Chambers' Encyclopædia, Unabridged*, omitting only the cuts, in fifteen volumes, with all the revisions of the Edinburgh edition of 1870, and with six additional volumes, covering American topics not fully treated in the original work:—the whole embracing, by actual printers' measurement, TEN PER CENT MORE MATTER THAN APPLETON'S CYCLOPÆDIA, which sells for $80. Following are the terms in detail:

For $12—CHAMBERS' ENCYCLOPÆDIA. A Library of Universal Knowledge, 15 vols., with additions on American subjects, 6 separate vol., 21 vols., in all, substantially bound in cloth, and THE WEEKLY TRIBUNE, 5 years, to one subscriber.

For $18—CHAMBERS' ENCYCLOPÆDIA, 21 vols., as above, and the SEMI-WEEKLY TRIBUNE, 5 years.

For $18—CHAMBERS' ENCYCLOPÆDIA, 21 vols., as above, and ten copies of THE WEEKLY TRIBUNE, one year.

For $27—CHAMBERS' ENCYCLOPÆDIA, 21 vols., as above, and twenty copies of THE WEEKLY TRIBUNE, one year.

For $26—CHAMBERS' ENCYCLOPÆDIA, 21 vols., as above, and THE DAILY TRIBUNE, two years.

The books are sent by mail or express at the subscriber's expense. The postage, if sent by mail, will be 10 cents a volume for the cloth edition, and 16 cents for the half Russia, which the subscriber will remit, if wishing them thus sent. By express, in packages, they can be had much cheaper.

We can furnish the books in other bindings as follows: Half Russia, gilt top, printed on heavy calendered paper, 45 cents per volume additional to our advertised prices. This is a very fine edition. The type is the same in both editions.

Eleven volumes of the work are now ready to be sent to subscribers, and the remaining volumes will be issued as rapidly as is consistent with good printing and binding.

A MAGNIFICENT GIFT!

WORCESTER'S GREAT UNABRIDGED DICTIONARY FREE.

THE NEW-YORK TRIBUNE will send at subscriber's expense for freight, or deliver in New-York City FREE, Worcester's Great Unabridged Quarto Illustrated Dictionary, bound in sheep, *edition of 1879*, the very latest and very best edition of that great work, to any one remitting:

$10 for a single five-years' subscription in advance, or five one-year subscriptions to THE WEEKLY, or $15 for a single five-years' subscription in advance, or five one-year subscriptions to THE SEMI-WEEKLY, or one year's subscription THE DAILY, exclusive of the Sunday Edition, or $30 for a single three years' subscription in advance to THE DAILY TRIBUNE, exclusive of the Sunday Edition.

For one dollar extra for postage, the Dictionary can be sent by mail to any part of the United States, while for short distances the express is much cheaper.

TERMS OF THE TRIBUNE.

Postage Free in the United States.

The Weekly Tribune.	The Semi-Weekly Tribune.
Single Copy, one year..................$2 00	Single Copy, one year..........................$3 00
Five Copies, one year............................ 1 50 each.	Five Copies, one year............................ 2 50 each.
Ten Copies, one year............................ 1 00 each.	Ten Copies, one year............................ 2 00 each.

And one free copy with every ten names. Papers comprising a club will be addressed to subscribers' names, and sent to as many different post offices as desired.

In making up a club, one Semi-Weekly will count the same as two Weeklies.

The price of THE DAILY TRIBUNE, including the Sunday Edition, is $12 per year, $2 50 for three months, $1 00 for one month. The Sunday Edition alone is $2 per year.

Specimen Copies, Posters, and Circulars sent free to any address.

Additions to Clubs may be made at any time at Club rates.

Address, THE TRIBUNE, New-York.

www.ingramcontent.com/pod-product-compliance
Lightning Source LLC
Chambersburg PA
CBHW030723110426
42739CB00030B/1356